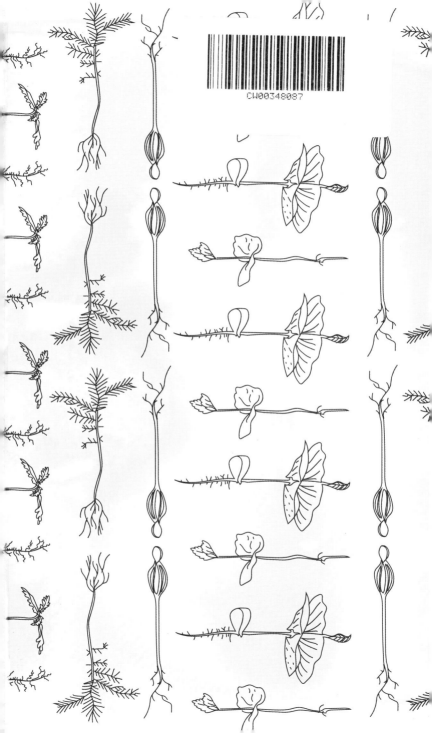

CW00348087

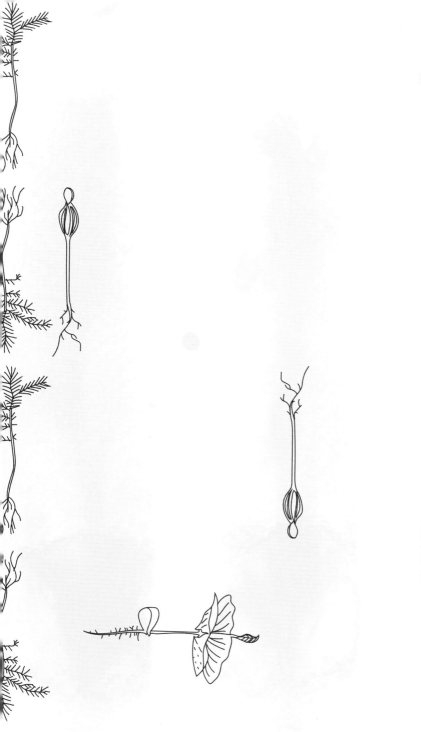

The Clearing
How We Live and
Die With Trees

ANDREW TODD

In Memoriam

Peter Todd
Suki
Peter Brook
Christopher Rådlund
Bruno Latour

Christopher Rådlund
Forest
oil on canvas

CONTENTS

Overture: Under-standing

Part One: The Seed

Part Two: The Canopy

Part Three: The Clearing

An Ending: Hornbeam

A Coda: Interself

Acknowledgements
Select Bibliography

Under-standing

Awaiting the trees, the living world was utterly flat, a microbe tapestry hugging the ground.

When trees appeared, they invented life as we know it: upright, varied, full of dreams, stories, cycles, kinship, and astonishing benevolence.

From 3 billion years ago life on earth took the form of an extensive, vibrant mat of microorganisms, crawling across sea beds and rocks, plastered on shorelines and volcanoes. This mat still exists in its 'natural' state on the north-eastern seaboard of America and in ocean floors; it is even tamed by us and deployed to clean up oil spills and to purify water. Over millions of millennia the mat started photosynthesis and produced our breathable atmosphere. Then, 400 million years ago, the mat was suddenly done with being flat. The production of lignin - a biopolymer which strengthens cell walls - allowed simple plants to form stems and to rise above the plain. The mat got innumerable erections, lusting to be closer to the sun.

Suddenly, life had a vertical dimension. Miniature proto-trees differentiated the layers of existence, creating varied characters of space: canopy, understory, roots. Beginning, middle, end. Things started to happen under the shade of the top dogs; instead of an undifferentiated morass of microbes, there were encounters and stories. Beings started to confront each other in their differences. Uprightness became the founding condition of life as we know it, of cycles of growth and decline, of shelter and association, of the production and consumption of nutrients from living matter.

It is not an exaggeration to say that trees founded our world and created the conditions into which we were able to emerge, 2 million years ago. Tottering on two feet, we stumbled into a terrestrial environment that was seemingly made for us, with material for tools, edible creatures and plants, water, capacities for shelter and adaptation to circumstance presented to us in abundance. Still today, trees continue to host us, producing much of the oxygen we breathe, fossilising into the fuel we burn in order to keep warm in a world where we are poorly adapted to live free and wild.

Like trees we are upright. We also have trunks, limbs, hair, skin, feet. We bend and resist, we change form, becoming - as we grow old - gnarled and knotty, stooped, surrendering to gravity. We and trees have individual characters, no two of us are the same. Trees have been personified, have taken on human agency, in our most important stories: they are active at the crucial junctures of all major religions, from Eden to Buddha's Enlightenment. They are protagonists in our great tales, from *Gilgamesh* to *The Mahabharata* to the *Divine Comedy*.

Trees play roles in our lives: they predate and outlast us, they surround and support us, they accompany us, albeit at their own pace. A bristlecone pine in California sprouted as the Great Pyramids were being built across the world. It is still growing. We all engage with specific trees, which become slowly mutating repositories of our quicksilver memory, companions who will know our great-great-grandchildren. My life is shaped by certain trees relating me to my father, who cared for forests professionally. His ashes feed the fig tree in the courtyard of the house where I am writing these words; I have inherited (and have to care for) his own plants, including the miniaturised subject of this book's first chapter. Trees are one of my ways back to him, and also forward into a life where I am destined to disappear in my turn, to return to the earth, to nourish other beings.

Trees become our most resonant artefacts: the conflagrated, millennial oak roof of Notre Dame. Christ's Cross. Exquisite Shinto temples which invoke the beginning of the world. Timeless Alpine cabins which season and ooze sap, grinding and groaning for centuries after construction. Stradivarius violins and cellos made of spruce, willow and maple, still unparalleled in their resonance after 300 years. As an architect I make wooden buildings in the full knowledge that they are partly alive and out of my control: I am a custodian and a composer of their energy and force. I set the scene, they act.

We live with, in and of trees. How we exploit them (and the contexts from which we take them) is a central question of our times, perhaps the key to our survival and happiness.

A few of us are still able to live in and with the forest, 'free and wild' as I said earlier. We will meet some of these people in this book. For most of us, however, human life is defined not by cohabitating with trees, but by destroying them and living in the voids we create. Human life takes place in clearings, the clearings we have made with our axes and chainsaws. In much of the world our spiritual narratives, our economic and political systems and our general worldview are predicated on looking down on these wooden beings that - in reality - loom over *us*. Human exceptionalism, bolstered by myth, marbles through every conscious and unconscious fibre of our thought, justifying grave incursions into the living matter which first welcomed us as naked, vulnerable bipeds.

By ripping open the fabric of forest ecosystems we have unleashed forces which were meant to be contained and continuous. These forces become volatile when decontextualised, and have a tendency to hunt us down in our clearings. Brutalised bats, chimpanzees and pangolins which should have remained sequestered and balanced in their sylvan habitats have leaked out microbes to which we are not at all adapted. By disturbing the forest habitats of other creatures, we risk making the world unbalanced for ourselves. As we expand our global clearing to increase our purchase on the planet, we risk undermining our very capacity to exist.

It has become a commonplace of the ecological debate that rewilding with trees is one possible remedy to this violence: we should fill in the clearings. As pragmatic human problem-solving, there is a danger that this may go no further than equipping the land with utilitarian oxygen pumps, disculpating airlines and oil companies buying them as utilitarian decarbonisation tokens. Such transactional simplifications mask the holistic character of the climate crisis. We have allowed ourselves to become unable to see the world as it is, with our place in it as only one amongst myriad actors of its wonder. To see the trees for the wood.

This book proposes that the all-engrossing character of the climate crisis impels us to look at trees simultaneously from multiple angles, as a fundamental part of the texture and process of life. Their religious symbolism, compressive strength, oxygen production, individual history, inspiration of dreams and so on are - to my mind - intricately related, and, when recounted in parallel, may produce new forms of understanding. This is the aim of this kaleidoscope-book: to generate a crystalline, cubistic sense of trees as multivalent beings and agents.

As co-upright beings, we must make a far better (and better-informed) effort to *stand with* trees in kinship, respect, and empathy. We must live within the chemical, physical, ethical, and philosophical limits of the world they have given us, rather than raiding it further from within the clearings we have already created. If we teach in order to learn, and write in order to read, this book is an attempt on my part to enable this *standing* by - first - *understanding*.

The Overstory author Richard Powers has described this process very beautifully:

> What's going to be required is a conversion of consciousness. I call it plant consciousness. We have to - one by one - begin that journey into interdependence, into reciprocal communal existence…. if you allow kinship, the question of 'you' becomes more permeable.

Richard Powers, 'Kinship, Community, and Consciousness: An Interview with Richard Powers', Emergence Magazine podcast: https://emergencemagazine.org/story/kinship-community-andconsciousness/.

This book records - and manifests - the beginning of my own journey towards a 'more permeable' me, towards 'plant consciousness.' I take this to mean quite the opposite of an anthropocentric projection of our emotions onto trees, depicting them as all sensitive and chummy; rather, our extended kinship requires new forms of empathy and attentiveness to forms of being and perception vastly different to our own. In my case, this journey predates me and will outlast me; I am curating a small part somewhere in the middle of things. The journey must address my specific roots and soil and must also branch out to unfamiliar terrain and entities, past, present and future.

The foundation of this book is grief. Grief is not negative: it is (when faced white-hot) a producer of heightened awareness and connectedness. I make no distinction between feelings of grief towards a raped, dying planet and feelings of grief at the loss of an individual loved one. Both are - or should be - intensely personal. Feeling distanced from the living world is the first step on the road to feeling the right to exploit it to the point of exhaustion. Or to feeling indifferent to such exploitation by others.

There are no charts in this book: we know the facts. We are a bit lost, however, when it comes to facing thoughts and feelings. We know, but we can't act accordingly, like Hamlet. Trees, however, can be excellent and instructive characters in our current drama: they are individual, global, social, mortal, useful, resonant, cosmic, earthly, urban, fruitful, frightening, sheltering. They have pseudo-human characteristics, creating and carrying relations between us - in the case of this book, between myself, my father and the vast world in which we eternally belong.

We will begin (as we already have done) with beginnings. Beginnings are repeated. Beginnings are false. Beginnings are weighty: politically, theologically, ideologically. Going back to a favoured or favouring beginning is one way to justify exclusion, murder, ignorance, exploitation. I wish to argue that we have to look afresh at our beginning stories as we are facing our ending: very often, the seeds of the latter are already sown in the former. Of course, it's not that simple. We will begin again and again, we will revise our starting points, retune them to current and past circumstances.

We will continue in the whole forest, disoriented, inspired, afraid, able or unable to survive and find our place. We will see the forest as a fault-line and battleground in our civilisational endgame, mostly wrapped around the planetary midriff in Central Africa and Amazonia.

Then we will consider how our clearings can be beneficent, how we can live within and without, how we can fashion the world from trees whilst remaining connected to them, living in balance with their gifts and needs. In so doing we will travel to Bavaria, Austria and Japan.

If art historical examples in this book are largely drawn from the Western canon, this is in large part because the worldview we have felt able to impose on the world has been formed by tools, thoughts and beliefs from this tradition. There is, however, a silent companion volume to this book, waiting to be manifested by others, which concerns the worldview of those who have lived in concert with our home, who have no blood on their hands.

(NXT)

one

the

seed

A Posthumous Bonsai (pinus parviflora)

'Nature…whose common theme
is death of fathers.'

–William Shakespeare, Hamlet,
Act I, Scene 2

Model World

When I was eleven I developed a passion for
bonsai. My father - who cared for trees, sites and
landscapes professionally - joined me in this. We
bought books and thrilled at finding in real life the
exact specimens we had studied in photographs.
We started to collect and cultivate our own bonsai,
including a young *Ginkgo biloba* in a white oval
pot, whose full-size, primitive, fan-shaped leaves
were laughably disproportionate to its tiny trunk.

My fascination for these model trees may well
have had something to do with a desire to remain
a child. I had gone precociously into puberty and
did not relish the upcoming metamorphoses, the
new rules, the changes of scale, mood, physique,
urges and behaviour of adolescence. I wanted to
stop time, which is very close to what cultivating a
bonsai entails. Perhaps not so much *stopping* time
as squeezing it, trammelling it, pretending that it
is not in charge of everything. There is something
slightly sadistic about bonsai, constraining plants
in a similar way to the rope constraints of Kinbaku,
Japanese erotic art bondage. There is - in fact - even

a sylvan form of bondage practiced on life-sized trees, called yukitsuri. Agile rope artists - such as my friend Kurato Fujimoto, master gardener at the celebrated Kenrokuen site in Kanazawa - shimmy up a pole placed alongside the trunks of ancient pine trees, and dress conical arrays of suspension cords to the lower branches, to protect them from breaking off under snow loads. In this case the constraint is caring and beneficent, but it is clearly expressed as a (very beautiful and poignant) imposition of Euclidean geometry onto living things.

I was deeply fascinated by the model-perfection of stunted bonsai, how one could practically starve a maple or oak and force it to produce miniature leaves, to bend it to one's will, to produce a microcosm utterly dependent on its creator-curator for survival and harmonious growth of form. This microcosm extended to the context, the footing of the tree, artfully exposing gnarled roots growing over mossy rocks, drawing water and nutrients from tiny pockets of soil in stones which were made

Kenrokuen
Gardens,
Kanazawa, Japan

to look authentic, asymmetrical, loose, artless - but which were, obviously, the product of minute control and forethought.

These settings reverberated with the full-size rocks and roots of the Lake District, which I was discovering at the same time (the beginning of a first lifelong infatuation with a place). This encounter was no less obsessive than my parallel fascination with bonsai, and was similar in some ways: after my first visit I made an elaborate chicken wire and papier-mâché model of Helvellyn as a mountainous tunnel for my train set in the attic. This urge to reduce, to capture, to master, to minimise, had a somewhat erotic charge, which would continue through my life in the professional pursuit of making architectural models in order to communicate volumes, scales, materials and settings both to myself - in the process of creation - and to users and patrons.

Whilst single-viewpoint computer generated images and fly-through films are pretty much the norm for representing buildings and urban spaces and convincing clients and public, they always lack something compared to a physical model. They are undemocratic, even pornographic: they dictate the terms of a distanced relationship intended to excite desire. They can also be reproduced on any graphic device, unlike a model, which has a single existence (and is often cumbersome). A model allows a consenting, physical, present engagement to be formed with a future building; the viewer chooses their subjective viewpoints freely and determines the conditions of their examination of the objective qualities of the scheme; the model generates a choreography between observer and observed which creates some democratic distance. There is no frame, no focal length, no blurring, no distortion, other than those supplied biologically and perceptually by the observing eye.

Larch tree roots,
Chamonix, France

There is a question of scale, of course: a large city model with tiny buildings merely reproduces the planner's viewpoint as a kind of organising force residing in the sky, concerned with property boundaries (and values) and iconic visibility, rather than pedestrian, street-level experience. I have experimented a lot with models big enough to insert part of the body - the head or even the whole trunk, particularly for theatres - and I had made one very particular model which showed both inside and out of a wooden theatre building for a presentation to Queen Elisabeth II. She expertly navigated the situation as a kind of ceremony based around the great significance of her viewpoint: she moved, bowed, peered, pointed and stood back to take stock, all the while subtly asserting her preeminence in the situation: she led the dance and posed intuitively for significant photographic capture of her attention and approving inspection. Her extreme gestural subtlety was rather more Japanese than British. (We will hear more of this event later: Elizabeth II was not merely regal, and had a specific relationship to forests and territories.)

Uproot

Whilst I remain totally fascinated by these bonsai-buildings, my child-self quickly lost interest in actual arboreal bonsai. I gave in to adolescence, but only up to a point; I remained trammelled, seeking approval as a good pupil, excelling academically. I would only break free of the bindings of conventionality at eighteen, during a liberating exchange residency in Southern California. I was no longer a model of my father. He, however, had to keep up our hobby. Bonsai is an extremely slow game: the tiny plants mature into their idealised, constrained forms at precisely the same proportional speed as full-size trees. The best specimens are hundreds of years old, formed by generations of custodians.

During our short burst of joint interest, we had acquired a fairly mature Japanese white pine, which bore the scars of training wires left too long on the branches by a careless former owner. This tree moved with my parents from the northwest down to Thornbury near Bristol (the city where they had lived and met as young adults). When my father finally tired of pruning it and coaxing its branches into a particular shape, he planted it in the ground of the lovely, intimate garden he created behind his very standard suburban house. The tree had landed, taken root, found its home, had earned - paradoxically - its freedom and independence by no longer being mobile.

My father's garden became a haven for him after my mother's early death and - for other reasons- after he had a serious stroke at the age of 72. A small, developer-delimited parcel of land, it became his horizon, an extension of his body, a theatre of his knowledge and fascinations, a miniature world of alpine plants, trees, ferns and spectacular flowers which he could curate, even with reduced mobility and perception.

He died in the dead of the year, on the night of the winter solstice, by the full moon, with a passing comet thrown in for good measure. His garden was in repose at that time, but it was obvious that the ongoing life it held would soon require intervention, decisions, adoptions and love. His own care had to be extended post-mortem by others, and the bonsai pine was a particularly difficult case in point: could it be persuaded to relinquish its freedom of growing in the earth, and become nomadic again?

Over the half-annual cycle which it took to engage the sale of his house, the question became more and more urgent. The buyers were informed

- legally - that this rooted life-form was not part of the property for sale. When I returned at the height of the year for final clearance, there was a distressing situation resulting from the absence of the gardener: weeds between pavers had reached waist-height, grass was meadow-like, catching stray biscuit wrappers discarded in front of the shop two doors down. And the feisty pine had put out candles which changed its profile; it even had cones growing where before it would have been continually tempered by its guardian. Its freedom had - in fact - been somewhat relative, dependent on the odd snip.

I had no idea how deeply it had rooted over perhaps a couple of decades. Friends and former horticulturalist colleagues of my father clucked at my uprooting idea and looked at me with a mixture of pity and concern: 'the root ball must be massive by now, how on earth will you take it away?'

Death means stillness. This was by far the strongest impression I took from the harrowing experiences of saluting the corpses of both my parents: life is *movement*, pulse, breathing, gesticulation, right up to its final moment. Thereafter, one becomes a shell, a mute object subject to other processes, without agency. One's coexistence with the world requires dynamism, acting upon it, ingesting it, breathing it in, exhaling and excreting it. Once this stops, one can do nothing but be reabsorbed into the world. At the end of my father's life - when he was unconscious and struggling to breathe after a massive final stroke - my only urge in his presence was to make as much noise and action as possible. I spent a day raucously singing along to Ella Fitzgerald and Frank Sinatra at his bedside, striding and dancing across his room, making speeches whose reception in his darkening mind remained only a mysterious, distant, unknowable possibility. I also experienced a significant upswing in all the life urges, becoming hungry, lustful, ambitious, hopeful, optimistic, generous, and intensely grateful and gracious towards all the hospital staff attending to this grim theatre.

According to statistics (proffered at that time by well-meaning friends), most people die alone and at night; they wait for their loved ones to leave, either because some residual consciousness wants to spare them further horror, or because they need a bit of Sinatra-free peace and quiet to get the job done. A friend who has twice been clinically dead on an operating table informed me that the overriding feeling was one of infinite loneliness and Anish Kapoor-grade infinite depth and blackness (this was also accompanied by experiences of warm, holy light). He maintained a surprising degree of control during the process, and purposefully decided to re-enter his body, experiencing this as a pure fact.

My father moved away for good in the dark of night, unattended. I went straight back to him at dawn and experienced the exceptional geometry of the dead. I felt the urge - again - to move, to salute, to exist in the axis of his body for a final time.

As soon as stillness takes over the loved one, all hell breaks loose for the living: bureaucracy invades, urgently requiring forms, permissions, signatures; one also becomes a short-term, frantic diplomatic news service, broadcasting constantly, generating protocols of who to call first and how; as principal witness one acts as a kind of priest, offering comfort as one breaks the news. Then the left-behind objects start to vibrate, clamouring for attention, for ethically appropriate ordering, removal, disposal, upcycling, recycling, redistribution and care. One by one, their aura must be recognised, weighed, and their fate as worthy (or not) of continued curation decided in thousands of emotionally-charged moments, often taking place in a dusty garage or a disordered bedroom. Once loose items like books, photographs and CDs have been categorised and arranged for further movement, larger items such as furniture have to be choreographed. On my final return - half a year later - I found it somewhat easier to occupy a house devoid of portable possessions, only barely furnished for marketing purposes, slightly depersonalised. However, when the fateful van-men came to take away - without courtesy or sentiment - the remaining bits of apparatus which accommodated the body to this rudimentary, conventional shelter, I experienced the voiding as a kind of expulsion from paradise. Mooching around the empty rooms, unable to sit or lie down, it was - as well - a crystal-clear flashback to our arrival without furniture when I was a bearded, long-haired eighteen-year-old, sulky after my return from California.

In the calm after this storm of expelled belongings, the bonsai pine remained proudly erect in the garden, at the apex of the cascade of objects, king of all he surveyed. I called on the help of a neighbour, a taciturn Welshman who moved in the same day as us in August 1986, fellow suburban pioneers on a new estate, he (and my parents) then a fair bit younger than I am today. Now ageing, he had (very unexpectedly) sobbed when I broke the news on the December morning, returning from the hospital. Now I needed to call on his elderly muscles and tendons to move the tree, the final act in this phase of this place.

I had started to dig - reverentially - a deep trench around the tree, occasionally needing to sever (with great trepidation) woody roots which had spurted out horizontally. I had no idea if the pine had put down a giant tap root which would require digging up half the garden; and the clock was ticking to get it done: a van had been booked to load up all the remaining treasure. The neighbour -thankfully- was less emotionally engaged than me with the situation, and far more pragmatic. He pushed the tree to and fro, revealing that it had not rooted deeply; indeed - as further archaeology revealed - my father had planted it in a fabric bag, limiting its growth, almost as if he had foreseen this moment. Swaying it, lifting it from beneath with a fork, it finally broke free and became a levitating body. Struggling with a surprising and awkward life-form, we became momentarily like the unbalanced crowd around the limp Christ in Michelangelo's Deposition, or His mother in the shatteringly moving Rondanini Pietà, bearing the unbearable weight of his spindly, stretched limbs through her stout legs. We - however - formed a wobbly, Anglo-Gallic, suburban version of this primordial scene. We laid the tree to rest in the largest locally-available pot - at an angle, its root geometry refusing to conform with the chosen container- and covered its twitching tendrils with soil. It was resurrected, captured, reburied, a model again more than a being, and ready for a journey.

Transplant

I am required to explain my own transplantation in order for you to understand what happened next with this cherished tree. Having been born in Dorset, continental Europe irrevocably entered my psychological makeup during a four-year sojourn in Germany from the age of 6. My father was attached to the British Army to care for their multiple sites in Northern Germany as a kind of cold war gardener, maintaining land occupied for geopolitical reasons: airfields, training grounds, forests, play-battlefields, all acting as a bulwark against the soviet threat, established a few hundred kilometres further east. He left his work manuals amongst his effects, revealing a heavy dependency on weed killers in 1970s site management protocols. Migrating afterwards through northwestern England, Los Angeles and Cambridge, my buds and leaves became an exotic, eclectic array; but I had left residual root matter on the continent. Freshly married to an American, herself also striving for fresh soil, we implanted in France as young professionals, having to develop knotty trunks and flexible branches in order to deal with buffeting from unfamiliar - and not always welcoming - conditions.

Roots can shoot down in search of water and nutrients in a matter of months, or they can lie dormant and shallow for years. In our case, we hardly noticed the gradual process by which we became anchored in one place rather than another. My wife's family was a kind of tightly-grouped copse: only one of her six siblings had moved away as she had done, and without leaving the country; the others were clumped together on the east coast, seeding seventeen offspring and (so far) four grandchildren. It was always a greater strain on her than on me to be away from familiar soil: the drama of long-haul air travel meant that visits 'home' could not be casual, light-hearted or occasional, as they were for me from Paris to Bristol. She did, however, have a particular attachment to my father, who recognised and nurtured her professional artistic endeavours from the standpoint of his own amateur activity.

France united our differently-bending trunks, providing a blank slate, a common soil where our senses of belonging and alienation grew in parallel; we were transplanted simultaneously, and the new roots were our business and nobody else's. It was a form of voluntary exile, comfortable and reversible compared to the fates of economic, political and climate-driven migrants. That is, until one June day in 2016. The result of the Brexit referendum happened to fall on the same day as the inauguration of a building I had made in the woods near Calais, a timber Neo-shakepearean theatre intended as a gesture of friendship towards Britain (whose microcosm-model I had showed to The Queen). Bad timing! Instead of delivering a smooth speech from the stage about the virtues of the project and the process, I angrily fustigated my compatriots (I had been denied a vote), and announced that I was now seeking French nationality, sensing that I belonged here and would not accept being uprooted against my will.

It now became urgent for us to anchor ourselves to avoid enforced migration, loss of rights, benefits, prestige and the positive identities we had painstakingly grown in France over twenty years. A few years earlier we had bought -on a whim, rather more mine than my wife's- an historic ballroom in a small medieval village in southern Burgundy. What had started as a dramatisation of midlife crisis slowly became our strongest anchor, our authentic roots. Shabbily joined to an incomplete set of adjoining buildings, the magnificent ballroom had been the centre of social life for the surrounding villages during the first third of the twentieth century. 5 men from the village - all highly active Résistance fighters - had been captured by the Nazis a few months from the end of the Second World War, denounced by a local. They never returned, and the form of the surrounding landscape changed as a result of the feminisation of the postwar farming population: a sudden massacre laid the way for a forest to grow back on unhusbanded land around the village. Our trees, ferns, brambles, mushrooms, badgers, foxes, rabbits, boars and deer exist like the ghosts of the hunted menfolk, the positive imprint of their absence. The ballroom building - augmented in uncertain spurts - also bore witness to this evisceration of energy, and slowly went to sleep as its former owner (daughter of one of the murdered Résistants) became too old to keep it animated.

Following the Brexit result, two things kickstarted in our own growth: we began the cumbersome paperwork to get our French passports, and we accelerated planning for the repair of our curious building. Using local stone flooring, gleaned drystone for walls, and magnificent solid oak panels sourced from the local forest, we joined up the inconsistent parts of the complex into a harmonious whole which was scaled to welcome festive events again. Taking a short sabbatical, I hesitantly became a cabinet-maker, and fixed the last door to the last cupboard during my father's final visit. It was a matter of great importance - especially in hindsight - that he witnessed the putting in place of the last twig of our nest; he could rest easy now that his migrating son had finally found a stable place in which to grow. It was not at all coincidental - for our sense of belonging - that the surrounding limestone landscape of rolling hills and hedged fields closely resembles his native West Country.

So it was obvious that the bonsai had to reverse-Brexit and find its place here, along with his other significant belongings. In fact, there was a certain fear in the early part of 2019 that the tree might need to be smuggled out rapidly in the case of a sudden No Deal exit from Europe. Its fate had become biopolitical, like the Anglo-German cold war forests my father cared for in the 1970s. Delivered by a barefoot Romanian van driver, hauled up the steps to the terrace, my wife and I deposed it again, trimmed its roots and foliage and settled it before a south-facing drystone wall. Having become shaggy and unruly, we tied its lower branches down in a kind of reverse-yukitsuri, as if it was yearning through the earth towards its native Japan. Our spatially-sensitive Japanese dog curled up in a perfect asymmetrical balance near its pot. Balance was restored by conscious arboreal transition.

Later, sorting my father's belongings, shaking a pile of loose papers earmarked for the bin, a card dropped out from among them. It was a kind of adoption certificate for the tree, recording it as a *Pinus Parviflora* imported from Japan at age 20 in 1983. My father had noted in his scrawling post-stroke handwriting that in 2018 (March, to be precise), it had been '55+' years old. In an even more hesitating hand, he had started to write another date for a note (this must have been later in the same year), but had given up halfway through. It is now my brother, and my son.

Suki with bonsai,
Blanot, France,
June 2019

Peter Todd,
Lephins,
Wantage, UK,
24th August 2018
(four months
before his death)

Fig-Birth in the Lake of Milk

The bonsai of the last chapter has one full-size neighbour in our small garden, also a migrant. She is a fig tree who grew up among serried battalions of commercial saplings in the lush Arno valley between Florence and Pisa. She was moved then to the Aosta valley to harden her up at a higher altitude, and was awaiting adoption when the word came through the grapevine of our local tree nursery that someone rather optimistic was looking for a five-metre-high specimen with the lowest branches at two metres fifty and a crown diameter of four metres maximum. We had almost given up looking (these were tricky criteria) and were prepared to plump for a Japanese maple instead; but the adoption papers came through, and she arrived at the midwinter solstice (a year to the day before my father died) in a huge pot, her branches wrapped up in pigtails.

We hoisted her over the neighbours' wall with a JCB I had flagged down in the street. I sat in the bucket of the digger and undid her hair-ties from above. She went 'ptoing' and shook her barnet. It was snowing and the hole prepared for her was filling in; there were a couple of minutes only to decide which aspect best suited the situation, and this was a fraught choice as her pigtails were still slowly unfolding into their resting, long-haired shape. The JCB driver had to scoot, so she settled rather by default, raised slightly above grade by the snow and mud that had accumulated, forming a kind of tumulus around her trunk when we filled in around the root ball (the tumulus was accidental and portentous, as well shall see later). There she was. I called Ron Henderson, a landscape architect friend (our adoption counsellor, and great aficionado of tree leaves and anatomy), so we could discuss names. We settled on Florence.

Florence had quite a spindly presence in her winter habits. Julie Bott, a winemaker friend in Condrieu, recounted how - after planting an entire vineyard of tiny twigs in austere, rocky land - the following springtime proved anxious: how could these measly fingers bring forth life? I felt the same way, and (for us both) the pushing through of buds and the gender-revealing first fruits of Florence was an occasion of great joy. The microfigs (actually introverted flowers) adorned the dry branches like tiny caper berries when my father made his final visit, the baby leaves - no bigger than a fingertip - striving for the sun.

Ron filled us in with some reading material on the portent of our adoptee. It turns out that she brought some baggage. As her leaves swelled in size into large, rough, triple-lobed solar panels, it became plausible to believe that Adam and Eve might have sewn them together (from the Tree of Life) to fashion the first clothes, as they became aware of their nakedness. The impossibly raunchy fruit was compared lasciviously to female genitals by Alan Bates' Rupert Birkin character in Ken Russell's film *Women in Love* (something embellished onto D. H. Lawrence's text, although you would have thought he wouldn't miss a chance like that…). Small wonder, then, that some biblical scholars have deemed the Tree of the Knowledge of Good and Evil to be of the ficus family.

Having done for the Son of Man, Judas hung himself on a fig tree, something rather hard to believe, as their branches are extremely elastic, bowing down in midsummer under the weight of fat fruits.

More auspiciously, Buddha attained enlightenment at the foot of a banyan (Bengal fig), and Krishna was born inside one, his mother sheltering from the tyrant Kansa. In Ancient Egypt the goddess Hathor had a fig tree whose branches were full of the bodies of the dead, taking the form of birds. Having been admitted to paradise, the fig fruit was their reward. The goddess Sefchet wrote on the tree's leaves the deeds and stories of the life of each dead human. One leaf per life. Can be used as underwear too.

Pleased that the new arrival was overweeningly pregnant with mythological agency, my personal favourite story became one from Georgia, which recounted that babies are held by its branches, which bend to lower them into a surrounding lake of milk, lifting them out to be plucked by their parents when ripe. As I soon discovered - when picking an underripe fruit - the fig produces a caustic white latex sap, used traditionally in Chad to stimulate human lactation by rubbing it on women's nipples.

Her new home was a success, maybe too much so. Florence shot out roots (we would see them when we dug - very carefully - to put lights in the courtyard -right) and got shaggy up top. In the first year she produced a large but rather insipid first harvest, and then gave up. In year three there was a terrible frost in late April which devastated the crops of our winemaker friends. Florence had her buds out, and my wife kept vigil in the courtyard with a night-barbecue intended to raise the temperature above freezing. It worked for the bottom half of the branches, leaving the look of a tonsured monk as the leaves emerged. Returning from holiday a month later, the top half suddenly decided to spurt upwards, and she looked for all the world like the lumpy bouffant of Nigel Tufnell in *This Is Spinal Tap*. Growing pains. And quite some personality.

When she gives forth, it's all at once, action-stations, plethoric stuff. Gorging on fresh fruit for days, we tend to run out of steam after the second batch of chutney and jam. There being five fig trees in the village, hardly anyone else wants the bounty either. Then, every February, I have the fraught task of pruning after the last hard frost, an exercise in four-dimensional divination, inevitably ending far from expectations, the final form unfolding according to climate and the energy levels of the tree in springtime. The pruning produces a set of antlers, as if there had been a tree-rut, a clash with destiny. Left to her own devices, she would swell and take over the house. Our shared life is a conversation, a negotiation, a dance, an origin renewed every year. And - as we shall see - it is also dusted with endings.

Fig tree roots uncovered during electrical works in the author's garden

Albrecht Dürer,
Adam and Eve
1504

Beginnings

Let's look more closely at how trees, wood and fruit appear in Christian originary narratives. There is more than one beginning in the Bible, which comprises two sometimes battling (and baffling) books from very different times.

Let's not start at the beginning of the beginning, but later, looking back to front. The New Testament Gospel of John Chapter 1 begins (in the King James Version):

> In the beginning was the Word, and the Word was with God, and the Word was God.
>
> The same was in the beginning with God.
>
> All things were made by him; and without him was not anything made that was made.

The New Testament God (speaking through the Gospel authors) did not leave pictures, sculptures or tunes to frame our lives. The Bible does not come with illustrations. Instead, he used language to get inside our heads, and his word originated our own speech and then gained its force through its embodiment in that form. We keep him present by using his gift, and by understanding his instructions. His authority passes primarily through semantics, rather than - say - ritual dance, song, pictures or iconography carved in wood. His claim to power is declamation, dictation, law, and this precedes all other creations (in John's interpretation).

John (or his coauthors) are echoing and giving roots to another claim, made in similar language by unknown writers, perhaps six centuries earlier, in the first book of Genesis:

> In the beginning God created the heaven and
> the earth…..
> And God said, Let the earth bring forth
> grass, the herb yielding seed, and the fruit
> yielding fruit after his kind, whose seed is in
> itself, upon the earth…
>
> And God said, Let us make man in our own
> image, after our own likeness: and let them
> have dominion over the fish of the sea, and
> over the fowl of the air, and over the cattle,
> and over all the earth, and over every creep-
> ing thing that creepeth upon the earth…..
> Be fruitful, and multiply, and replenish the
> earth, and subdue it…
> I have given you every herb bearing seed,
> which is upon the face of the earth, and every
> tree, in the which is the fruit of a tree yield-
> ing seed; to you it shall be for meat. (KJV,
> Genesis 1: 1, 11, 26-29)

We are thus entrusted with the delegated destinies
of everything from beasts, fish and trees to caterpil-
lars. 'Dominion' may mean - according to gentler
exegeses - 'stewardship' or 'authority' or 'care,' but
it can mean something altogether different to the
profit-minded ears of a Bible-belt farmer. He might
hear, rather: 'the Big Guy says it's ok to make hay.'
Likewise, thoughts of 'dominion' could fire up the
clear-cutter's chainsaw in Amazonia.

Man is created twice in Genesis: he has to be made
again - with an interesting nuance - in Chapter 2
(most historians regard Chapter 1 as having been
added after Chapter 2, just to simplify matters):

> And every plant of the field before it was in
> the earth, and every herb before it grew: for
> the Lord God had not caused it to rain upon

the earth, and there was not a man to till the ground.

But there went up a mist from the earth, and watered the whole face of the ground.

And the Lord God formed man of the dust of the ground, and breathed into his nostrils the breath of life, and man became a living soul. (2: 5-7)

Seemingly, God loses the plot: rain happens without his intercession (as a result of vegetal evaporation), and he hurries to create Adam both as a result of, and to intervene in this process: the earth calls out for husbandry, it needs upkeep, and its husband is formed from the clay made by the first independent act of the ecosystem. It's also worth noting that Chapter 2 has no mention of dominion or subjugation of the created world by mankind. God then makes Eden (a planned, planted garden rather than a wild landscape) for Adam with 'every tree that is pleasant to sight, and good for food' (2:9), including the aforementioned tree of life, and the other which is famously out-of-bounds.

Already - in its first three pages - the Bible displays its beauty (as a montage, a collective, contradictory text), and also its dangers as an ideological buffet to be picked over according to whatever view you should wish to justify and reinforce. For our purposes here, its inconsistency is of a piece with human nature: we really don't know why we're here, and the scriptural God leaves us an awful lot to figure out for ourselves.

We need our own means - including graphic representation - to make sense of these stories.

Old-growth larch forest,
Val Ferret, Italy
(see p. 254)

43

The Errant Cross
(Aleppo Pine)

The Gospels and Genesis - far apart in time and worldview - have sometimes been entwined together with externally-supplied joining matter, long pieces of stretchy ideological elastic, or intricate tendrils which try to tether the New Testament to the stories of the Torah in order to make a convincing whole. Trees play a central role in one such story-vine. *The Legend of the True Cross* is not scripture, but a story from the 13th century, from a book of saints' lives by Jacobus de Voragine. It has acquired considerable authority (if not dominion), in no small part through good visual PR. Piero della Francesca made it the subject of his 1447 masterpiece fresco cycle in the San Francesco Basilica in Arezzo, a sort of graphic novel illustrating how wood grown in Eden ended up wandering across time and space to make Christ's cross.

The story recounts how, upon Adam's death at the age of 931, his son Seth plants in his mouth (during the burial) a sapling cut from an apple tree from the Garden of Eden, one of God's original 'pleasant to sight' trees, which will eventually grow into the cross of Christ. The first man is buried as the soil of Christ's future undoing, the first shoot of the new covenant emerging from where Adam's voice (his apple…) once was. Grown, cut down and turned into a beam for a bridge, the timber is recognised and venerated by the Queen of Sheba (as she crossed the bridge); she then informs King Solomon that this member will dis-member the realm of the Jews by killing their future Messiah. Solomon has the bridge dismantled and buries the beam, but it is later exhumed by the Romans, and put to its fateful use.

Further chapters in Piero's visual story include the future Christian Emperor Constantine's dream-vision about the cross the eve of the battle of the Milvian Bridge (in which he was incited to fight under the standard of the Christian God as a path to victory - and then his imperial ascension) and the Christian-Persian battle between Heraclius and Khosrau (both were one-sided, foregone-conclusion triumphs for the 'home' side in religious terms). These battle scenes closely recall the contemporary paintings of the San Romano Battle by Piero's colleague at the Montefeltro court in Urbino, Paolo Uccello. The best of Uccello's three paintings of this subject (now in London's National Gallery) depicts the scene of devastation somewhat as an artificial forest, with lances piercing the air in a random pattern, and broken lances and corpses under the battle like an artificial undergrowth of fallen trees and bodies. Uccello also depicted (in another painting in Oxford's Ashmolean Museum) a memorable and eerie hunt through a forest, of which, more later...

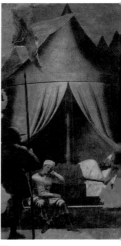

In another of Piero's scenes, the cross is discovered in Jerusalem by Constantine's mother; it possessed miraculous powers (she is also shown starving a Jew down a well in order to extract the knowledge of its whereabouts). This actual wood (thought to be Aleppo pine rather than applewood) was then splintered into hundreds of fragments which are venerated to this day. One of them was kept in Notre Dame Cathedral, near my home in Paris, and was rescued in conditions of great danger by firemen during the conflagration of the building's famous roof-timber 'forest' on April 15th 2019.

Emperor Constantine's Dream

Piero's cycle is a confusing mishmash full of leaps in time and place. It does not read like a straightforward graphic from top left to bottom right (although the story could have been told this way,

The Death of Adam

Adoration of the
Holy Wood and the
Meeting of Solomon
and the Queen of
Sheba

49

more or less as I have). Instead, he constantly disorients us. None of the segments are arranged in temporal sequence (although there is some pairing through opposite-facing positions). Hardly any of the individual frames depict a singular event: they are often split or multi-screen, non-simultaneous events depicted in the same frame with a cutting device within the scene. This is often an actual tree standing in the middle: the fateful apple hogs the composition of Adam's burial, relegating the narrative action to the very bottom left, pushing the precedent scene of the ailing Adam to the right. Besides the omnipresent cross and its timbers, there are tree-avatars in almost every scene, such as the lances in the two battle scenes and the central pole holding up Constantine's tent. This tent, a circular shelter with peeled back flaps, recalls the later composition of the Madonna del Parte, where Mary is shown spreading a genital-slit in her dress inside a tent identical to Constantine's, another reference to Christ as the second Covenant, the fulfilment of Old Testament scripture.

Piero seems to be saying to us that origin narrative is utterly elastic, looping and bouncing backwards and forwards, cycling like the seasons of my fig tree. And the arboreal being that binds it together for him is - graphically - the central character, rooted in and nourished by the deepest past, capable of hiding and reemerging as a shapeshifting agent of beginnings and endings.

The First House. And the Next First House.

In early summer, working away on this book in my eyrie office on the balcony of the historic ballroom which is part of our house, I realised that I was not alone on my perch. The warm air moved through the huge windows of the ballroom, allowing darting swallows to enter, race around, chatter, pause, and leave. After a while I noticed that they were not leaving, and the chatter was increasingly focused below my balcony. Looking carefully on the lower ledge of the I-beam supporting the structure, I saw that architects were at work. In repeated trips, the canny swallows were fetching building supplies (mud mixed with saliva and bits of straw and branches) and starting to stick them together to make the foundations of a nest, in which they could hatch their offspring and house them during the summer, until they were able to fly back to North Africa in the autumn.

I loved their company and their high-energy speech, but I realised that we could not cohabit for long, as the windows would need to be closed for long stretches (in case of absence, or rain). I therefore had to respectfully cast them out, encourage them to look elsewhere, with a very heavy heart. Before they left, I thanked them for inspiring my work by reenacting a primordial story from a book then on my desk, written more than two thousand years ago.

Marcus Vitruvius Pollio was a Roman engineer and architect who wrote the only treatise on building to have survived from antiquity, his *Ten Books of Architecture* of between 30 and 15 BC. Vitruvius (who died somewhere around 15 AD) was therefore a contemporary of Christ, a coincidence which did not escape later commentators who sought to apprehend his pagan thought (not without difficulty) for their own monotheistic aims.

He concerns us here because the forest is a central presence in his own origination story: for Vitruvius, home, architecture, society, human behaviour, speech, all result from the accidental clearing of the primordial forest by fire.

By a further coincidence his work reappeared into Western thought at about the time of Piero's fresco cycle. Having been known through Carolingian transcripts in the middle ages (although largely ignored) it attained a new lease of life after being discovered in 1414 in the library of the monastery of Saint Gallen (in Switzerland) by Poggio Bracciolini, a Florentine humanist who saved many decayed and forgotten tomes from antiquity. Its first printed edition - in 1486 - was therefore widely known just 45 years after Piero's fresco cycle, and was assiduously studied by Piero's contemporaries Leon Battista Alberti and Leonardo da Vinci, the latter leaving us the most famous illustration of the text, the curly-haired, intensely frowning, sinewy Vitruvian Man spreadeagled in a circle and square.

Vitruvius - relatively unnoticed in his own lifetime - exists for us as a sort of time-loop and time-capsule: he is important mostly because of the rarity of his work, and the timely circumstances of its rediscovery, just as western Europe was rebuilding its intellectual foundations on the limping, uneven legs of Christendom and Antiquity. Having apparently written his work in retirement, in homage to Emperor Augustus - it might have been a kind of vanity-published professional memoir, a pat on his own back after a busy life of service making aqueducts and such like - Vitruvius would probably be amazed that his breezy description of the beginnings of architecture - being the only one we have to work with - now wreaks havoc with our entire intellectual history. By barging in on our approved origin stories, it gives a false start to the clock of Judaeo-Christian progress.

Writing from the time of Christ, zapped forward to and then digested directly in the Renaissance, his own attitude to our emergence from nature has been reread (and often misread and distorted) for hundreds of years as a central founding text, usually slathered in a Christian sauce. I find the *Ten Books* particularly interesting - in our current condition of being stupidly at war with 'nature' - because they present a rather subtle and fluid account of how we come to exist as upright, aware, communicative, mobile creatures, profoundly modifying our world.

For Vitruvius (in his second book, Chapter One) it all starts with a fire in the woods:

> The men of ancient times bred like wild beasts in woods and caves and groves, and eked out their lives with wild food. At a certain moment it so happened that the thick, crowded trees buffeted by storm and wind, rubbed their branches together so that they caught fire: such men as witnessed this were terrified and fled. After the flames had calmed down, they came nearer, and having realised the comfort their bodies drew from the warmth of the fire, they added wood to it, and so keeping it alive they summoned others and pointed it out with signs showing how useful it might be. In this meeting of men sounds were uttered at different pitch, to

which, through constant daily exercise, they gave customary value to the chance syllables. Then, by pointing to the things in most common use, they began to talk to each other because of this accident. Since the invention of fire brought about the congress of men, and their counsel together and cohabitation, and since many people now met in one place, and had moreover been given a gift by nature above that of other animals, that they did not walk with their heads down, but upright, and could see the splendour of the world and the stars; and since they could make whatever they could wish with their hands and fingers easily, some of that company began to make roofs of leaves, others to dig hollows under the hills, yet others made places for shelter in imitation of the nests and buildings of swallows of mud and wattle. Then, observing the construction of others, and by their own reasoning adding new things, as time went on they built better dwellings. Since men were of an imitative and docile nature, glorying in their daily inventions, they would show each other the result of their building; and so, employing their abilities in competition, they gradually improved their judgment. At first, setting up forked posts, and putting withies between them, they finished their walls with mud. Others built walls out of dried clods, framed with wood, and covered with reeds and leaves to keep out rain and heat. When, during the winter, the roofs could not resist the rains, they devised gables, and smearing the inclined roofs with clay, they made the rain water run off.

Morgan (1960)
p. 38

In this brief passage, Vitruvius sets up the terms of future centuries of debate about animacy, agency, semiotics, semantics, linguistics, cuisine, craft,

54

ecology, culture, style and tectonics. If only he knew the trouble we have seen, the battles we have endured because of his blasé originality, the hot air (and stones) wasted in the battles of ancients and moderns in the 17th century, the contortions undergone to make this appear suitably Christian.

Let's slowly pick this feast apart.

Just as the Biblical God was caught napping in Genesis 2 by the first rain - by the immediate and unexpected agency of his self-made world - so Vitruvius depicts humanity as being gently surprised out of its original baseness by the independent actions of the forest. You will note that the fire which

Cesare Cesariano, illustration of Vitruvius, Book II Chapter i.

starts humans thinking and gathering is not stolen by a Prometheus, nor delivered in a spectacular lightning-bolt by Zeus. Instead, the origins of humanity lie in a somewhat improbable, even banal friction of branches in wind leading to sparks and the combustion of the woods. As a likely adherent of stoicism, Vitruvius paints us as initially fearful (in an animal-like way), but innately capable of mastering our anxieties in order to understand the world and apprehend its forces. These 'wild' people become the first foresters, cutting wood to add it to the fire in order to regulate the warmth which provided an hospitable nexus for shared perceptions, grunts, attuned musical groans, pointing things out and eventually developing language and social organisation thanks to this common physical context. There are no gods - pagan or otherwise - involved here (fire is a rather random 'gift' from nature) nor is there an heroic conduit for sacred knowledge (like Moses). Vitruvius is very relaxed about the beginnings of society, presenting it as something natural, inevitable and locally-produced without grandiose intercession. The forest clearing - he seems to be saying - is all we need to live: a place in which to gather, develop consciousness, associate, communicate and make.

I'm slightly uncertain about why Vitruvius feels mankind suddenly needed to stand upright (it appears to be a question of congregation and mutual facing, but presumably this could have been done on all fours as well). Notwithstanding, being able to look up and around (rather than merely down at the ground grubbing for food) opens up celestial thoughts and prepares the way for the sacred geometries and statures which would rapidly fold into his narrative of the architectural orders and human-divine proportions (like Leonardo's Vitruvian man). Our bipedic posture also frees up the hands to be crafty, and this gives rise to the fashioning of shelters in imitation of animals, such as nests and burrows. Vitruvius describes us, indulgently and fondly, as cooperatively competitive, egging each other along and wishing to communicate, to admire and be admired for our efforts and ingenuity. He is hardly a social Darwinist of the Chicago School.

This two-legged brainstorming morphs into erect and rectilinear shelters which start to resemble authentically 'human' architecture: a vertical wattle and daub box, improved - for purely utilitarian reasons of rain runoff - into a rudimentary temple shape with the addition of double pitched roof. From that point, Vitruvius can get into detail, explaining subsequently how Greek temple architecture evolves into stone from wooden construction techniques (like these forked forest trunks), a further imitation game.

Animal Builders

Before we rush headlong into anthropocentric history I would like to turn back and dwell a little longer with the animals who show us the way. It seems to me that my ballroom swallows -and those invoked by Vitruvius- have something very important to tell us. Animal architecture had to wait a very long time to be taken seriously again after Vitruvius; at least until the latter nineteenth century with the Reverend J G Wood's *Homes Without Hands* and - closer to our own time - a series of studies by the ethnologist Karl von Frisch and the contemporary Finnish architect Juhani Pallasmaa. What if, Pallasmaa argues in his essay *Animal Architecture*, we are not the only architects? What can we learn from the extraordinary variety and ingenuity of the works of non-human selves? How are they different from us - if they even are?.

Pallasmaa makes apparent a world of untold ingenuity and richness. Animals, he reveals, use tools (from crushing stones to tiny picks to the wheel made by the scarab beetle); they produce high-performance materials (paper was created by wasps millions of years ago; spiders' thread is three times stronger than steel, and light enough to be used as a wind-borne aerial transport for its creator); they create complex habitats which are adapted to site conditions (the wasps' nest which changes structure from chimney to roof beam to wall; the critical regionalism of a specie of African termite which builds differently from one place to another); and they build differentiated architectonic elements just like us (hinged doors with a Gaudi-esque handle for the trap-door spider (Nemesia caementaria); separate toilets for the marmot; translucent windows for the tropical True Wasp). Perhaps most impressively, animals have created habitats with levels of environmental precision which make us look positively leaden. The termite colony is predicated on a system of passive ventilation tubes which makes the Pompidou Centre look less than primitive with its exo-guts spilling everywhere and going rusty every twenty years; the honey bee can control the temperature of a hive to within two degrees Celsius, using gangs of beating wings as a heat regulator; the ant goes outside in large numbers and stores solar heat in its own dark body when the hill needs warming up; the wasp brings water into the hive to cool it by evaporation.

This world is presented with little polemic, except a few explicit parallels between human and animal vernacular techniques, such as dung and straw combinations. Pallasmaa states laconically that, generally, the 'higher' the animal, the clumsier the architecture; he lets us draw our own conclusions about our environmental fall from grace. The Yemeni cities like Sana'a which survive almost

without water and outside energy, and ingenious-
ly husband their meagre resources, can be seen as
parallels to this world of frugal non-human builders, with which we cannot directly communicate.
What Yemeni builders appear to have in common
with our animal kin is the application of a greater
level of ingenuity in proportion to the scarcity of
a resource. (One could also apply the same for-
mula in reverse to current developments in places
such as Dubai and Las Vegas, where utterly inhospitable conditions have nonetheless served as
the scene for the most overblown and wasteful
architecture).

For Pallasmaa, a shared ingenuity is not enough to
welcome animals into the club of actual thinkers;
their works are techno-determinstic. He quotes (in
the epigraph to his exhibition catalogue) his friend,
the late Norwegian architect Sverre Fehn in this
regard: 'the bird's nest is absolute functionalism be-   Pallasmaa (1995)
cause the bird does not know it will die.'

Architectural historian Joseph Rykwert has been
a pioneer in collecting and revealing origin stories
in architecture, particularly in his book *Adam's
House in Paradise*. I cited Fehn's statement to him,
somewhat expecting him to concur that humans
are distinct, special, reasoning creatures, upright,
conscious, separate from the rest of nature. He re-
plied: 'I wouldn't be so sure about the bird not   In conversation
knowing it will die.' A very wide (and very recent)   with the author,
range of thinkers in various fields feels the same   2009
way, regarding our relations to the whole ani-
mate (and also inanimate) world as conditioned
by a much greater degree of reciprocity and in-
terlinking than anthropocentric Judaeo-Christian
thought has allowed for over the last two millennia. It is perhaps not a coincidence that our attention is turning to the inestimable wonder and
complexity that surrounds and supports us just as

59

we are snuffing it out. These questions have also begun to infuse the arts, with multimedia creator Tomas Saraceno unleashing his collection of spiders in the vast Palais de Tokyo contemporary art centre in Paris, giving them (somewhat) free rein to spin and weave structures which are certainly artful - and very beautiful - but also unstable and ephemeral. His 'artists' were sometimes disobliging about their habitats created for the art cognoscenti, destroying them and rebuilding them before the eyes of alarmed aesthetes; the whole point is that they are in charge, we are spectators (although Saraceno stage-manages and carefully presents their creations). His blockbuster exhibition also showed some of the amazing structures Pallasmaa recounts, including a lengthy thread which floats on air, acting as an ethereal form of transit; elsewhere in the exhibition he presented a human version, a sun-responsive hot air balloon requiring no combustive energy to take flight.

Pallasmaa further develops the link between animals and the vernacular in his 2005 book *The Eyes of The Skin*. The book begins with a ferocious attack on the hegemony of the eye in contemporary society, and a plea for a more holistic, integrated approach to human perception. 'The inhumanity of contemporary architecture and cities,' he writes, 'can be understood as the consequence of the negligence of the body and the senses, and an imbalance in the sensory system...this sense of estrangement and detachment is often evoked by the technologically most advanced settings, such as hospitals and airports...modernist design at large has housed the intellect and the eye, but it has left the body and the other senses, as well as our memories, imagination and dreams, homeless.' Vernacular architecture, by contrast, is described as representing a 'total fusion' of the senses: it is 'guided by the body in the same way that a bird shapes its nest by movements of

Pallasmaa (2005) p.19

its body. Indigenous clay and mud architectures...
seem to be born of the muscular and haptic senses
more than the eye.'   Ibid.

So perhaps the major distance between ourselves
and animals is indeed our Vitruvian, biped character
with our handy hands (subject, by the way, of another book by Pallasmaa, *The Thinking Hand*). We
are just qualitatively more agile with our extremities
than birds or dogs, who shape their nests and dens
with circular, pushing gestures of the back. Indeed,
Vitruvius presents us with a graded, shaded appreciation of our development away from the forest:
there is no divine 'aha!,' no magic finger infusing
things with the life-force. He recounts our beginnings as having been rather collegial with the rest of
the world, and goes on (after the passage I quoted
above) to provide his first-hand accounts of how - in
his time - it was still possible to observe 'primitive'
constructions of the type he ascribes to animal mim-
icry, in places such as Marseille.

Guess what? We can still see such things today, especially in societies where a market of high added
value goods and components has not penetrated
and destroyed non-money-based local circuits.
Vernacular architecture continues to be made from
ultra-local materials transformed and assembled by
social groups from shared knowledge (rather than
by contractors and professional specialists - like
myself - according to codes which exclude common knowledge). A fair proportion of the world
- perhaps the majority - live in beautiful structures which are closely adapted to local climates,
made with readily available resources (including
waste products). Far from being 'primitive,' such
buildings are in many ways more advanced, better adapted to circumstance, than our ultra-slen-
der skyscrapers, super-heated, uninsulated villas,
deathless, dayless casinos and so on, which actually

Kestrel delivering food
to its nest (illustration
from the catalogue of
Pallasmaa's Animal
Architecture exhibition)

Entomologist Walter R Tschinkeland
with an aluminium cast of a
Pogonomyrmex Badius ant colony

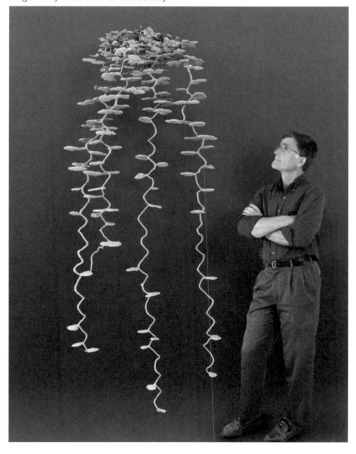

depend on a vast hinterland of resources in order to remain upright and inhabitable.

Our problems really start when we have to clear someone else's forest in order to live. We become - in Pallasmaa's terms - 'homeless' in our homes, exiled on our main street, when we begin to live - materially and ideologically - beyond the capacities of our own forest clearing.

Outcast

Like most origin stories, Vitruvius has been largely taken to signify not how things got started, but how they ended up - with clear legitimacy - *like us* today. His readership and frame of reference were Augustan Roman with the obvious inherited continuity of Greek architecture; he also (as I have noted) was familiar with various forms of vernacular architecture, which would certainly have been preponderant in Ancient Rome, just not downtown. Hence he drew on both, but with an emphasis on 'harder' constructions, which would have been where he earned his keep professionally. It would not take long in the life of his *Ten Books* to obfuscate, to erase, to turn the page on the 'soft' subtleties of his story, and to cherry-pick the bits which best correspond to a human-centred worldview. Pretty soon, it would all be about temples, orders and styles, often to enforce a conservative worldview (such as the attempted imposition of Donald Trump's preferred neoclassical 'federal' style). The providential forest, its chatty humans and ingenious animals are long-forgotten on the marbled avenues of Washington D.C.

Filarete (whose given name was Antonio di Pietro Averlino) was an early Renaissance architect and writer, a contemporary and colleague of Leonardo and Piero. We owe to him - as part of a team -

64

the Sforzesca Castle in Milan, in which Leonardo frescoed an immersive, mysterious forest (of which, more later). Filarete is important for our story right now because he was one of the first thinkers to attempt to relate (or even conflate) Genesis and Vitruvius as forest-based origin stories asserting humanity's primacy in the world.

He published a sprawling 'book of building' which was mostly concerned with bigging-up his prime sponsor (the Trumpian warlord duke Sforza) through the theorising of an ideal, duke-branded city, Sforzinda. In one passage on beginnings we see a curious double-page spread: on the left, the naked Adam (looking for all the world like Leonardo's Vitruvian Man after a lengthy hiatus from the gym) is being expelled from Eden by God, irate at his having tasted from the Tree of Knowledge of Good and Evil. Notwithstanding that Genesis 2 had featured the first gentle precipitation as the initiator and agent of planetary growth, Filarete's Adam is shown as caught out for the first time by the extra-paradisiacal rain, the elements revealing his nakedness and unsuitedness for the fallen world. Expelled from Eden, he needs shelter for the first time, and improvises a roof over his head with his hands, as drops of rain fall from a clump of clouds in the sky. Oddly, he is standing on a rocky shelf or island, seemingly trapped, rather than freed from the confines of Eden. He bears the legend 'Vitruvius Adam.'

On the right hand page there is an illustration of a construction specifically described by Vitruvius ('forked posts…and withies'), organised in a rectangle. The forks in the tree trunks support the principal beam-logs, the secondary members resting on the primary. It is practically a primer in traditional wood construction (especially Japanese), with minimal transformation of the trees, whose secondary shoots have been lopped off. It is a knotty frame which serves no apparent purpose, having no walls or roof; an abstraction enclosing pure space, something you might see in an art museum by Giuseppe Penone, rather than the urgent and pragmatic structure elucidated by Vitruvius.

By arresting this construction at an intermediate, unfinished stage, Filarete emphasises its frame, the relationship of column to beam, the construction ideology questions which would resonate through the 17th century (when science emboldened architects to overthrow the 'rules' they had inherited and worked to without too much questioning). And of course, these questions continue to preoccupy us today, with no consensus (but plenty of entrenched positions, especially from conservative quarters) on what constitutes the beautiful.

Filarete,
The origins of
architecture,
in Trattato di
Architettura

Leonardo da Vinci was deeply concerned with Vitruvius, having hunted down one of the first existing manuscripts in Italian - in Pavia, with his friend Francesco di Giorgio Martini. Francesco

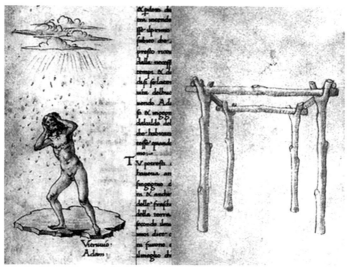

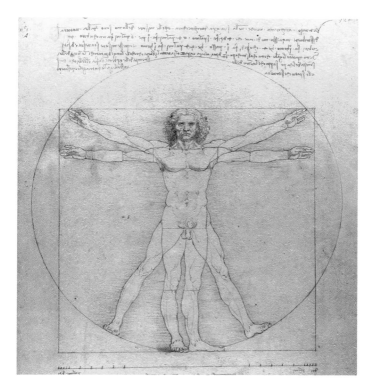

- architect of the ducal palace in Urbino, where Leonardo would later stay - produced several illustrations of the splayed Vitruvian man, squished into a church plan with his head at the apse, overlaid on the facade of a renaissance church (itself based on the Roman volume of a law court or basilica). When Leonardo came round to producing his own drawing, the protagonist (probably a self-portrait) would be fierce, confident and strong, unlike Francesco's relaxed characters. Leonardo knew what he was doing: his figure (whose body is bracketed by further sub-proportions) represents the human as microcosm relating upwards to the city and cosmos, and as the source of all positive beauty and rules of proportion. Alone, male, strong, looking as muscular as

Leonardo da Vinci, engraving of Vitruvian Man

a temple or Filarete's trunk-frame, he stares out at us in defiance of the gentle, interspecies sociability of the forest clearing in Vitruvius' text.

Langourous Laugier

Marc-Antoine Laugier was a French architect, philosopher and sometime Jesuit priest active during (and central to) the rationalist enlightenment in the middle of the eighteenth century. His two *Essais sur l'Architecture* were immensely influential for neoclassical architects such as Blondel and Boullée (author of an unbuilt and spectacularly overblown cenotaph to Isaac Newton). Fitting into the slipstream of the previous century's heated arguments about breaking from the 'positive' beauty provided by Vitruvian models, he felt able to chill out in his own origin narrative.

Laugier describes a man wandering contemplatively through an agreeable woodland (we can presume a scholar or priest - perhaps not a construction worker). Nature is presented as being almost-all-right: the lawn is soft and sun-dappled, there is a gently-flowing river, a warm breeze. The man shelters from strong sun under the leaf canopy; then, when it rains, he hurries into a cave, and muses on how things are really not so bad: nature offers him just about everything he needs in this life of nature-aesthete leisure (there is no talk of fire, of food, of other humans). However the cave is not all mod cons: it is dark and musty. Time for a makeover:

> He leaves the cave determined to compensate by his industry for the omissions and neglect of nature. Man wants a dwelling which will house, not bury him. Some branches broken off in the forest are material to his purpose. he chooses four of the strongest and raises them perpendicularly to the ground, to form

a square. On these four he supports four others laid across them; above these he lays some which incline to both sides, and come to a point in the middle. This kind of roof is covered with leaves thick enough to keep out both the sun and rain: and now man is lodged. true, the cold and the heat will make him feel their excesses in this house, which is open on all sides; but then he will fill the in-between spaces with columns and so find himself secure.

Laugier (1775) p. 2

So far, so Vitruvian, at least in tectonic terms: like Filarete's diagram (and following the original Roman récit), Laugier raises a sort of trunk-temple in a woodland glade. In the illustration of this scene, in which a female personification of architecture points languorously - a bit like Michelangelo's Adam - at the structure, the uprights appear to be living trunks, still in the ground with lush lower branches. Laugier was naturally writing with his contemporary audience in mind, who were preoccupied with purifying the architectural orders of columns and entablatures, stripping things back to basic, rational elements (structural loadings were about to be calculated for the first time), enveloping space with rhythm alone, supporting pediment and roof in an 'authentically' classical manner without fussy Roman arches and brick walls. His attitude to the natural world is ambiguous. On the one hand, he decries nature's 'omissions and neglect' of his needs for total comfort, shortcomings which can only be overcome by human endeavour; and then - having gone to a lot of bother - he remains fairly relaxed about being open to the elements in his creation, describing full enclosure (in non load-bearing infill elements) as a bonus to be added when time and funds permit in phase two, once he has reclined some more by the babbling stream. Architecture - in Laugier's account - is semi-neces-

70

sary, important first of all as a mental construct, as an assembly of approved elements to make primal forms. And it certainly does nothing to bring people together, to get them talking, to broaden their language, to have them collaborate, as it had - fundamentally - for Vitruvius, in his greatly extended origin-process.

Laugier uses the pretext of beginnings to reinforce his own status quo, preaching to the converted about a rather temperate, unproblematic context where a leisurely, lonely dweller has few problems to solve. Nature is semi-beneficent, pleasant, picturesque, mildly bothersome. It doesn't sound like our world at all.

Previous page: Marc-Antoine Laugier, the personification of architecture and the primitive hut

Doxi and Epergos Mansplaining Their Origins

Nineteenth century French architect Eugène-Emmanuel Viollet-le-Duc unexpectedly found himself one day in an Alpine crevasse, the unwitting subject of an experiment about the limits between the 'human' and the 'environment.' He had spent all his free time in the last decades of his life circling Mont Blanc, drawing and measuring it from all angles, single-handedly producing the first comprehensive map of the Massif (you might say he was a bit *driven*; he thought sleep was a waste of time…). Having fallen into an icy chasm during one of these high-energy jaunts, he found himself holding the end of a broken rope, resting on a snow bridge which had formed itself partway down the abyss. Knowing that it would take several hours for help to arrive (with a new rope), he began engaging mentally with the calculations concerning his chances of survival. How long, he thought, would the snow bridge resist the heat of his body? Then it occurred to him -with a certain horror- that 'nature' would win this race, freezing his buttocks long before he himself posed a threat to the environment.

This may have been a case of unconscious vengeance by the mountain. Thousands of metres above his perilous perch, mighty Mont Blanc may have gotten wind of his utterly mad idea that time had denatured the mountain, removing its virile structural beauty, slumping its spire. He had proposed (to the French Geological Society, obtaining their enthusiastic assent) that it was time to restore Mont Blanc. Thankfully (perhaps), Viollet-le-Duc never got into the specifics of this, how many billions of tons of rock would have to be moved up 4,000 metres: it would have made Stonehenge and the Pyramids look like a game of ping-pong. Nevertheless, just the fact of having -and breathing- the idea tells us a lot about him and his time. Obsessed with the gothic as a 'rational' architecture of balanced forces and economy of means (and voided of its ethereal, tree-canopy symbolism), his writings strongly influenced modernists like Frank Lloyd Wright and Le Corbusier. You could say he was a kind of prophet of the Anthropocene, the kind of guy the Koch brothers might have liked to fund in a quest to rewrite history, stop the clock and deny change - whether man-made or natural.

Viollet-le-Duc was the obsessive architect of the mid-19th century renovations of Notre Dame. Back then, he had been given absolutely free reign to amend and 'improve' the crumbling monument, replacing and refacing weathered stones, remaking half of the timber roof 'forest,' tweaking flying buttresses, and adding the famous spire over the crossing, featuring a selfie-sculpture (as Saint Thomas, patron saint of architects) descending from heaven towards the Paris pavement. He was 25 years old at the time of getting the job; today he might have been the ultimate Instagram influencer, an archi-Kardashian imprinting his own identity wherever he could. At the time of writing, the long-dead Viollet-le-Duc has finally become a mass-media figure, constantly in the news and subject to lively debate concerning the merits of replacing his (conflagrated) impositions on the medieval building. It's quite a conundrum: in an ancient building, there are no origins to return to: every part of a building this old will have been retouched, tweaked, attacked during a revolution or two, scraped by the elements of its original gaudy polychromy (which we would probably find awful today). When he began work on it, it was in a long decline (decried by Victor Hugo) following its fall from grace as a secular Temple of Liberty after the 1789 revolution. Nonetheless, the brief didn't necessarily call for the kind of absolute lifestyle-makeover he had in mind. It is therefore interesting to hear our contemporary commentators (usually of a conservative timbre) virulently defending his transgressions as part of a unitary, sacred heritage. Time levels all things.

You may well have guessed from his presence in this story that Viollet-le-Duc could hardly resist concocting his own origin-myth. It reads like a bad misogynist-colonialist tract filtered through Jules Verne, with a sprinkling of Vitruvius on top. His *Histoire de l'Habitation Humaine* was written - late in his life - for a popular audience, and featured an adventurous time-travelling duo, Doxi and Epergos, who journeyed through architectural history, occasionally improving things a bit as they passed through. Naturally, they call in on the first dwellers, yellow-skinned, straggly-haired, saggy-breasted, long nailed and utterly unable to produce an enduring home. Their attempts to live under branches spread with mud and animal skins are doomed to failure. Just as Notre Dame had been saved from itself by a spot of time-travel, so our intrepid duo set out to civilise the differently-tinted savages of yore, by - incidentally - creating the first gothic structures. Take that, Vitruvius! His original Roman *quadratura* is historically side-stepped by Epergos shimmying up a sapling and bending it towards another, which -attached at the apex- becomes the first building *and* the first gothic pointed arch. Then the natives are exhorted to clear the forest and add further young trees in a pointy cone-shaped shelter which -clad with branches and mud-sheds rain far better than their own meagre efforts. Naturally, the whole tribe wants one, presumably leading to social homogeneity and conformism.

Viollet-le-Duc,
'The First Building'

Frankenstein Island (Prickly Pear, Eucalyptus, Banana...)

Amongst my hoarder-father's effects I found an un-usually exhaustive and uncharacteristically well-or-ganised dossier of mementoes relating to one brief voyage. The trove comprised maps, notes, books, dozens of photographs and even boarding passes, tea towels, postcards and drink mats. This docu-mentary trail recounted that in February 2003 he had travelled on an RAF Tristar (seat 17K) to a speck in the Atlantic, one of the most isolated, primitive and curious places in the world. In one of his final professional acts, he was sent to survey trees on Ascension Island, a place which is part-Eden, part-hell, part-foreign planet and part-terraformed biotope, and which teaches us a great deal about the rest of our terrestrial context by virtue of its exception. Only 88 square kilometres in size, it points the way towards both the beginning and the end of the world.

These neatly encapsulated messages from him are entirely in keeping with the nature of the is-land in question: sailors used to leave messag-es in bottles there, hoping that a passing ship would relay them to loved ones on the other side of the world. Ascension is a global and cosmic in-between, destined by its extreme remoteness to relay news and communications, and to serve as a unique observation-point and microcosm. Roughly equidistant between Liberia and Brazil, 8 degrees south of the Equator, it sits 1,300 km northwest of Saint Helena. Noticed in passing by the Portuguese admiral Joao da Nova in 1501, it was an unwelcoming sight, a fresh volcanic island

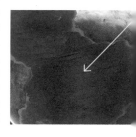

bereft of vegetation except for scant endemic ferns and flowering plants, and home to vast flocks of seagoing birds. It remained uninhabited for three hundred years until its proximity to Saint Helena made it the only logical outpost for protecting the incarcerated ex-Emperor Napoleon from potential French raids to free him from his island prison. This role lasted only for the six years that the deposed despot survived, but it resulted in the establishment of a rump civilizatiion on the deeply inhospitable Ascension.

Fifteen years later, in 1836, Charles Darwin stopped by at this rudimentary outpost of the British Empire on The Beagle's journey back to England. It was here that he intercepted a message informing him of his sudden, enormous fame back home. Darwin despised the island, dubbing it 'a cinder,' and making note of a possible idea for its future transformation.

Ascension has remained a point for observation and for the relay of secret and globally-important messages. In 1877 it was used by astronomers David and Elizabeth Gill to confirm the distance between earth and Mars during a particularly close encounter between the planets; in the late 1970s it was used to maintain contact with the first Viking probe on its way to actually visit the red planet.

In 1982 it achieved short-lived fame as a refuelling point for British air forces on their way to the war in the Falklands, further south off the coast of Argentina (it had served the same purpose for the American forces on their way to Second World War skirmishes in Africa and Asia; the Americans built the runway). Today, further than anywhere from the mass of humanity to east and west, it is one of only four land-based points which keep order in the Global Positioning System, regulating the locations of billions of unseen devices and persons. The idea which took root in Darwin's mind during his brief, barren sojourn was communicated to his chief collaborator in botanical matters, Joseph Hooker, shortly after The Beagle's return home. What if, Darwin proposed, this roasted piece of basalt could be made to support abundant life, and demonstrate the processes of evolution from an almost blank slate? Could we generate an artificial climate at the same time, using imported trees to incite moisture to stick around their heads and organic matter around their feet, creating a tropical rain forest? Could it be made to live from a patchwork of assembled pieces, like Frankenstein's monster? Until then, only a few giant pseudo-scorpions had previously been able to survive in cracks in the petrified lava, and the Island was punishingly hot and dry. Darwin wanted to engage in the act of terraforming, of creating inhabitable terrestrial conditions from their contrary.

Seven years later Hooker was able to reconnoiter on Ascension on his way back from Antarctica with James C. Ross's expedition. Another three years later he began the curious process of dressing the island with specimens previously plundered from other British colonies and corralled in Kew Gardens (which was then directed by his father). Once a month, ships discharged a cornucopian cargo of Ficus, Eucalyptus, Bamboo, Agave, Bougainvillea, Aloe, Prickly Pear, Blackberry, Banana, Coconut and Date palms; there were even Norfolk Island Pines to grow replacement masts for ships. Five thousand trees were planted between 1862 and 1874, some coming directly from Australia and South Africa. They were left to fight it out amongst themselves in this context, to organise their own diplomacy according to their most appropriate context. The bamboo scaled the heights of Green Mountain, the island's highest point at 857 metres, and happily grew into a tropical cloud forest, with a few mates from the *guajava* genus.

The island's existing animal bounty included turtles which arrived there to lay eggs, exhausted after crossing half the Atlantic. After their exertions they became a prime ingredient in British Naval Officers' soup. The same went for the Wideawake birds' eggs, another delicacy for humans, which pushed the birds to nest in inaccessible, craggy parts of the island. The native fauna was soon augmented by new arrivals destined to complement the fruit and veg offerings (and indeed to feed off them): pigs, goats and donkeys were joined by unintentional guests such as cats and rats. For a while the cats ruled supreme, taking over large swathes of the island. The donkeys also claimed their freedom from the farmyards of the tiny village, and roamed through the mountain shrubs and trees, increasing in number. They gave a new lease in life to the mesquite tree by disseminating its seeds in their nomadic donkey doings. The plant world was no less prone to jostles and sudden upsurges in particular species: the prickly pear looked at one point set to dominate all, until human agents unknowingly introduced a particular moth which liked to nibble their fruit.

It is hard to resist the temptation to recall here the Biblical Eden of Genesis 2, in which God sees rain happen for the first time somewhat independently of His will, making the clay from which humans would then be formed. Even He is subject to terrestrial agency and caprice, to the self-sustaining processes and will of Gaia. Ascension was - like Eden - created from almost nothing, willed into being in a short time, and populated with a basic cast of characters who quickly began to interact in unforeseen ways. Perhaps the whole point is that - even on a 'cinder' such as Ascension, or the feisty Eden of Genesis 2 - we are somehow in the middle and the muddle of things, rather than at a pure starting-point.

The Bible and Darwin have -unjustly- contributed far too much to our *muddle*. Just two words - the previously noted 'dominion' (from Genesis 1) and 'fittest' from Darwin (as in 'survival of the..') have been misappropriated and distorted to justify our current course - a course which can now only result in the exhaustion of the earth, its transformation into a scorching, early Ascension-like hell. Darwin's 'fittest' - used to justify the oppression of the disadvantaged, the weak and the poor - was never intended to mean 'strongest.' It denotes, rather, the best-adapted to a given circumstance, which might be delicate, hybrid, freakish creatures, fish who feel the urge to flap up onto a beach, or Ascension Island donkeys who would rather wander in the mountain bamboo groves and eat guava, than remain tied up in a pseudo-English garden. Darwin did not intend us to understand that you get ahead only because you eat your neighbours.

Ascension - as a terraforming experiment - has compressed the millions of years usually required to create a functioning ecosystem into a couple of hundred years characterised by cat wars, donkey dominance and rapid swings between dominant tree species. Islands (real or imagined) are a typical setting for experiments on humans, whether serious (*Robinson Crusoe*, *The Lord of the Flies*) or stupid and degrading (*Love Island*). On Ascension, however, the island itself is the star, the subject and agent of crazy forces set in motion by humans. My father's journey there was to act as one of a tiny cast of arbiters who -once in a while- minutely record the state of play, in case adjustments are required. This process is necessarily beyond the scope of a single human life: Hooker never saw the results of his mad experiment, and my father's observations about mesquite, bamboo and guava have already outlasted him, to be taken up by others who may or may not get his message. Trees are far bigger than us, physically and temporally; we intersect with their lives as if we were apes swinging through them; they carry on regardless (unless -of course- we chop them down).

My father was particularly interested in the status of the few endemic ferns and flowers of Ascension, which were overwhelmed by the arboreal rave party disembarking since the 1850s; he was also deeply moved by the (now protected) turtles and their extraordinary will to live and reproduce. He was deeply proud to walk in Hooker's footsteps and to add a new layer of understanding to our rather odd relations with our terrestrial roommates in this laboratory setting. I am enthralled to have discovered his time-capsule relating to this trip, not least because he actually taught me comparatively little about trees during his lifetime. I have taken up the task of getting to know his mind after it has closed, following the traces of the many books and papers he left behind.

Posthumously, in a kind of tree-time extending beyond human talk, I am able to intertwine his investigations with the urgent and recent noises emitted by my artistic and scientific colleagues who are engaged in a battle to understand the myriad implications of the climate crisis. What is currently at stake is whether we will follow the macrocosmic transformation of the earth backwards in time to the microcosmic original cinder of Ascension. Terraforma / Terrarupture…

We all exist today in a state of grief, grief for the disappeared, or for the about to disappear. But grief is not negative: it is, rather, state of heightened awareness and connectedness which forces us to face, clear-minded, the splendour of life and the world, and moves us to continue to observe and curate it with ever-greater love, care and energy.

Peter Todd surveying vegetation on Ascension island (photographer unknown)

two

the

canopy

'The here -where we are- is an enigma.
We are all lost.'

Bruno Latour

Cited in Thorsen (2017), p.154

Peter Todd
navigating

Ghost Trail Through the Forest of Dean

Tottering Tattoos

My father kept 59 British Ordnance Survey Explorer Series 1:25,000 maps, nearly all of them crumpled from extensive use. They are now in my library in Burgundy, a jaunty orange splash of colour amongst the grey spines of his biographies of the likes of Stravinsky (two of them..) and Stan Getz. The maps cover a good swathe of southern Britain, with some territories in the north, especially the Lake District. They are not objective guides to the terrain, they are diaries. Opening the sheets covering the Forest of Dean, one of the oldest and strangest tree-landscapes in the country, I found, in the centre of the woods, a convoluted loop delineated in yellow highlighter ink, cleaving to contour lines along a ravine, undecided about following a ridge from Blackpool Bridge to Bullock's Beech, or staying in the deep valley bottom. Never emerging from the forest, the yellow trail turns tightly to take in Thorny Tumps, Serridge Horn and Patton Stone. Another loop, more casually traced in faint pink, turns around Mallards Pike Lake.

My father being a determined and active character, I have no reason to believe these were theoretical trails: he almost certainly walked them, having planned them out carefully in advance. He was always out, sometimes alarmingly AWOL, and it was impossible to keep up with the details of his peregrinations as they happened. The map traces now have to speak for themselves. The Forest of Dean walks perhaps reflect a certain introverted mood: the lines never break into clearings, although they could have done. He apparently wanted - on those days - to remain in the company of ancient trees with a short perspective in front of him. Perhaps he also wanted to remember his last outing there with my mother - when she was wracked with cancer - which concluded in her falling into the mud. She was very large at that point, bloated with steroids, and he was unable to lift her. They struggled and rolled around and became completely covered in wet mud, a tragic situation which - being so close to actual mud-wrestling - led them to explode in laughter. I'm not sure - and now have no way of knowing - if this ending consciously recalled a beginning for them, in which - during his horticultural studies - he asked her to sit at the wheel of his tractor as he examined a problem beneath, with a warning to her not to touch any pedals. My mother, an extremely nervous driver who hit an old man during her first attempted driving test, and didn't retake it for thirty years, must have touched something: the tractor kicked into gear, squishing my father into the (mercifully soft) mud like a scene from a Roadrunner cartoon. She careered into a hedge across the field, screaming with fear that she had crushed her fiancé. But for a previous rainfall in

that field, or a passage of clustered, trampling cows in just the right place, I might not be writing these words now.

Rather impressively, all of his maps bear similar luminous slug-trails, some of them very extensive. I know that he walked the Cotswold Way in its entirety as a way of coping with grief after my mother's death; over three maps you can see the chunks in bright yellow, separately executed but proudly linking together. I sometimes followed him along his fluorescent lines. Living in the United States during my graduate studies, where rights of way across farmland are practically unknown, and the landscape is often featureless for miles around, I craved this dense, layered, muddy, woody, often prehistoric landscape every time I returned home, and these walks became rituals of reconnection with a deeply complex place peopled by ancient trees and early human constructions.

Ghost Trail of Blood

There is now a ghostly quality to the fluorescent trails he left behind, echoing disappearing tattoo-dots made by his feet, and the ephemeral imprints left by his and my mother's bodies in the mud at the beginning and end of their union. Peer past his own floating traces and it becomes apparent that the map itself is equally shifty and insubstantial, despite purporting to represent *terra firma*. Obviously, the vegetation precisely delimited on these large-scale sheets grows and dies back every year, and is subject to husbandry and felling, to changes of boundary, to the appearance of clearings. Take a similar fluorescent line across the contemporary Brazilian forest and you might find the map is out of date almost immediately, fields of soybean for distant cattle opening up like vast wounds where one expected a dark canopy of palms and the chatter of monkeys. My own maps of the Alps, which I have visited two or three times a year since 2003, are also distressingly out of date, glacier snouts now patently far behind their graphic locations, height data off by hundreds of metres, paper-white expanses now covered in grey rubble as the ice mass vanishes before our eyes. The spot where I first stepped onto the Mer de Glace now bears a commemorative plaque (detailing that year's level) above a spindly ladder leading down to the current glacier, far below. My own ghost-steps of that first expedition are now suspended high in the air.

Even the familiar, fusty, musty Forest of Dean, sylvan setting in the final Harry Potter book and in several Dennis Potter stories, is too protean to be meaningfully captured by the authoritative Ordnance Survey. Explorer Sheet OL 14 fails to register the influence of the underground on the surface of the woods, namely the coal deposits which made it contested ground in the 19th century, spawning mono-purpose settlements such as the depressingly-named Cinderford; nor do they explain the tumult of 1808, when 4,500 hectares of common land were due to be enclosed for private exploitation, giving rise to bloody riots, eventually suppressed by the army, rallied from as far afield as Plymouth. The shapes of the woods seen from above on the maps are -on the ground- traced in blood.

The map is a whitewashing, a false witness, a dumb affidavit of erratic process. A clue to this corruption is in the name: ordnance. The initial impulse for laying out the land on sheets of this size was for mastery of terrain, to know where to orient airborne munitions. Distance, angle, arc to destination. Boom.

Mer de Glace, Chamonix, May 2017
plaque showing 2003 level of the ice

The Upside-Down Forest

Frédérique Aït-Touati, Alexandra Arènes and Axelle Grégoire take issue with the dangerously misunderstood limitations of conventional cartography in their brilliant book *Terra Forma*. They attempt to set the record straight - or to stir things up - on a number of matters, including the supposed objectivity of the sky-view projection, the paradigm-shift of the Global Position System and the failure of maps to see the earth in depth and in flux.

They depict the origin of conventional maps (like my father's) as scenes of story-telling, organisational systems of knowledge uncovered through exploration, added to successively by each new explorer in the respective terrain. The earth is fleshed out, filled-in, furnished in all its details by observation. Each map represents a bounded territory, a rectangular-framed sky-view generated by an inexistent, disembodied eye. The framing avoids the geometric projection problems of global maps which have to unfurl and flatten the orange-peel of the planet, usually to gravely distortional effect, making (in particular) conquered and exploited lands appear smaller than they are in reality (the case - in particular - of Africa in the Mercator Projection).

The author-explorers don't bother to go as far as global distortions in their account: it suffices for them to look down and around your feet to see that even small maps lead us astray. As I intimated above, *Terra Forma* argues that conventional maps are not good at process: they see the world as a container or platform frozen in a snapshot. They stifle the fact that the earth surface we occupy is literally alive, the tiny inhabitable thickness which sociologist Bruno Latour calls the 'varnish' of life's 'Critical Zone'. The Critical Zone is not just an animated and shifting stage, it is both scene and action, the product of all the life-forms which occupy it, as well as their only conceivable context. Whilst not being a neutral or objective account of the life-surface, 'standard' cartography serves to flatten and negate non-western approaches to annotating the territory: an Aboriginal Australian, who might find their way through a map organised equally by experience, story and significant features, would find our maps opaque and useless, just as we -lacking their specific insight- have to decrypt and translate their poetic diagrams of the territory.

Our authors follow this caveat about flat maps with even more circumspection when it comes to new ways of orienting ourselves in space such as the Global Positioning System, or GPS. By tracking our position from space (and bouncing off the earth-station on Ascension Island visited earlier by my father), we become totally individualised in a universal set of abstract, gridded coordinates overlaid onto the territory like a crisscrossed pie crust. The principal purpose of GPS is to move us without friction, mishap, disorientation (and with a minimum of local knowledge) from A to B in a measured time. This fluid efficiency has the effect - for our authors - of erasing and suppressing 'stories, assemblages and multiplicities.'

The book proposes a series of remedies, new forms of documenting and recounting space. They subvert GPS with their idea of the 'Gaia Positioning System,' a rather more elastic and resistant network which shifts between the relative and respective standpoints of the full range of the 'animated' (living things and objects) who constantly make and remake the world with us and around us. Their idea is a bit like stretchy dough, a somewhat sticky, resistant substance that maintains an overall form whilst responding to local forces and energies. They show experiments in constituting the territory through the movements and diplomacy of different species, each eking out their own space in cognisance of what other guys - badgers, foxes, birds of prey, human hunters - might be up to.

More radically, when it come to the misrepresentation and misunderstanding the air we breathe and the soil beneath our feet, they propose a totally flipped representation of the world, in which the atmosphere (in reality, a finite and fragile epidermis, which seems infinite because we look through it at the stars) is turned to the centre of the earth. Trees grow inwards and 'downwards,' their roots pointing outwards, the resources necessary to life - which we fail to see correctly in their thin-spread fragility - turned into an introverted globule of air and organic matter, palpably, easily exhaustible, corruptible, pollutable. Like a lung or stomach. Like medieval Viking representations of Yggdrasil, the world-tree whose roots and trunk are reciprocal, uniting heaven and earth through the trunk. And also like Hungarian architect Imre Makowecz's extraordinary installation of a tree with denuded roots (exhibiting its airy and earthy duality), growing through a plane of glass in his installation at the 1992 Seville Expo.

We observe this representation from the side, allowing us to understand scale and layering as more important for life than distribution of elements on a plane.

Sociologist Bruno Latour - who collaborated intensely with our authors - took some of their magical illustrations as the backbone of his performance-lecture 'Inside.' The title resonates with the last drawing I described, in which the earth is introverted ('like a glove,' in Latour's own words). For the philosopher, it is deeply problematic that our perception of the planet has -for centuries- placed us apart from it, as unique viewers with a special, privileged perspective. We have projected ourselves to exist as other, outside, blithe, disengaged, un-affected by the natural world and fellow humans - especially anchored, traditional societies- except inasmuch as they stir feelings of the *sublime* for us.

From a lecture in Huringy, France, August 23rd 2020

Recounting a flight to Calgary during which he sees what seems like a screaming face incised in the melting ice of Baffin Bay, Latour reflects that the climate crisis has had the effect of flipping the con-ventions of art and historical history on their heads, like *Terra Forma*'s trees:

> I was in this plane, watching this thing screaming at me, and I was not outside an-ymore, because my own kerosene-powered journey - to a minuscule but quantitatively significant extent - was actually the cause of this precipitated melting of Baffin Bay. So I was not outside, I was *inside* the spectacle. I've been on this plane many times, and every time I've felt something which we could call the sublime. But this time I didn't feel that way, because to feel it you need three things: you need to be outside, you need to feel very small compared to what you see, and third… you have to feel immensely big - morally speaking- compared to stuff outside…. I know that - myself - I'm minuscule, but we humans know that we are the equal of, we are now overpowering this ice pack, so the asymmetry is totally reversed. And the other asymmetry…we feel, with tears in our eyes, that we are morally very low.

From the playtext of 'Inside,' English adaptation by Andrew Todd

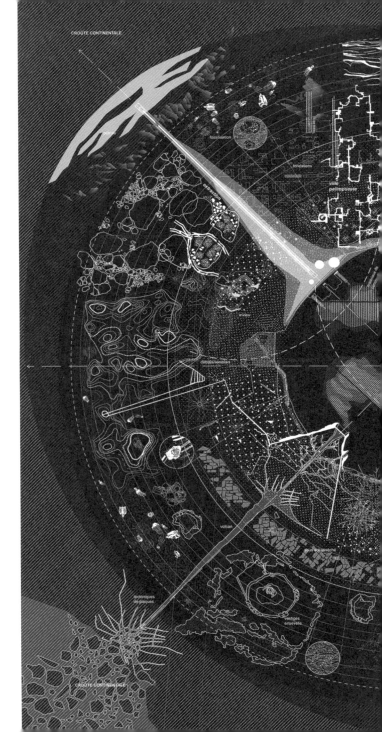

CROÛTE CONTINENTALE

fossilisation

fondations

ville
palimpseste

extraction

décomposition

volcan

rivière asséché

tectonique
de plaques

vestiges
enterré

CROÛTE CONTINENTALE

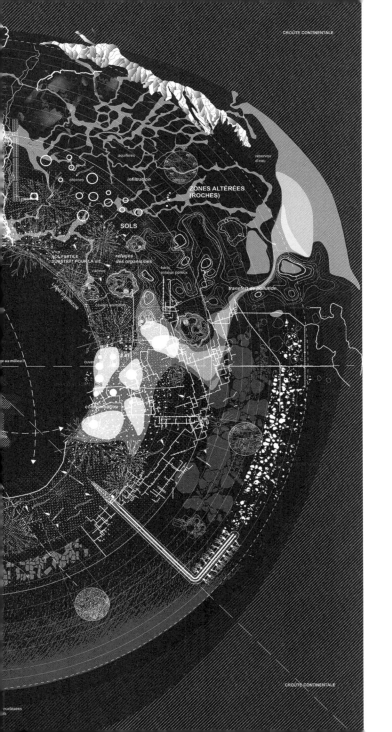

aquifères

réservoir
d'eau

crêmes

infiltration

**ZONES ALTÉRÉES
(ROCHES)**

SOLS

**SOL FERTILE
SUBSTRAT POUR LA VIE**

*refuges
des organismes*

karst
réseaux poreux

un horizon

transfert de pollution

cavités animales

cuve

e au milieu

contamination

nucléaires

He goes on to fustigate against the 1970s 'Whole Earth' image of a lonely blue planet, which was supposed to have united us in empathy as regards the finite character of our home. For Latour, however, our self-perception as being on this marble has only served to foster divisions over the last forty years, precisely because it is a false image of how terrestrial life exists. It presents our world as a rounded, harmonious, self-sufficient, resolved Platonic whole of heft, harmony and thickness. What should have brought us together has in fact driven us apart. In reality - as we have seen with *Terra Forma* - life only really exists in the furtive, fragile, trembling vertical space between the bottom roots of a tree (where the bedrock starts, under a tiny film of organic soil) and the crown of the leaves, the highest part of any ecosystem (surmounted - arguably - by the flight zone of birds).

Latour relates globalist, whole-earth thinking to the modernist and neoliberal projects, which depend entirely on a vector powered by unlimited resources, something which our planet is utterly unable to provide. Inwards rather than outwards, a retreat within national borders, a shunning of a sense of shared responsibility and belonging, has seen a resurgence of right-wing nativist politics; however, these are often used as a fig leaf to disguise an expansive neoliberalism. Latour proposes that we recuperate terms like 'soil' from the far right, and rediscover our home planet as something that is neither global nor local, but in constant vibration between the two poles. We need to know *how* and *where* we stand, what exactly our 'footprint' or dependency on the world is, individually, as citizens. We must also be aware of, and empathise with, all the other footprints marking - like my father's ghostly map-feet - the fragile Critical Zone. This necessary act of rediscovery based on detail and attunement to the horizontal web of relations is - for Latour - no less of an upheaval than the huge paradigm shift which occurred in the 16th and 17th centuries as the European conception of the world expanded to include the 'new' continent of the Americas.

Photograph by Bruno Latour of the Canadian ice sheet from a flight to Calgary

The Vanishing
Vanishing Point

How we see the world, how we project ourselves into it, how we survey it, how we consume it with our eyes, hands, feet, tools and weapons, is, therefore, a central question of our time. I want to look at this with a certain historical spread, and my story concerns an astonishing early Renaissance painting of a dark forest.

In this story, we shall shift our viewpoint from that of the disembodied, all-seeing sky-eye of conventional cartography, to the complex, challenged, passive-active, inside-outside view of the individual eye seeing things 'in perspective.' In so doing, I will also have to resituate autobiographically, to see eye-to-eye with my teenage self.

Painter Paolo Uccello was a contemporary and compatriot of Piero della Francesca, seen earlier depicting the peregrinations of an ür-tree which would slay the Son of Man, shapeshifting from applewood into his future Cross. Uccello and Piero may well have stayed together at the court of the Duke of Urbino in the period around 1465: Duke Montefeltro gathered the greatest minds of the age in his isolated hilltop city, including Raphael, Leon Battista Alberti, and Francesco di Giorgio Martini; Leonardo da Vinci - to whom we shall soon turn - built the Urbino citadel's ramparts and access stairs shortly after Montefeltro's death.

In Piero's paintings and frescoes - as we have seen - there is often a tree occupying the centre-ground. In the first image of the True Cross Cycle, Adam's death is marginalised to the bottom of the pictorial space in deference to a central tree (which may

be a representation of the apple tree being insert-
ed into his dead mouth - as a sapling - in its later,
fully-grown state). In the *Milvian Bridge* scene, the
Emperor Constantine is separated in the picture
from his vision of the cross by another centralised
tree, mirroring Adam's on the opposite wall of the
chapel where the frescoes are painted. In other images (such as of the *Veneration of the Queen of Sheba*), the scene has a column cutting the picture in
two, a sort of avatar of the former trees; this device
is also used in his Urbino *Flagellation of Christ.* In
the London National Gallery *Baptism of Christ*, a
tree takes up most of the picture, standing slightly
aside for Christ, who occupies the centre under a
hovering dove representing the Holy Spirit.

Piero and Uccello lived at the threshold of the
Renaissance, and wavered in their work between
the techniques of linear, 'accurate' depth perspective (which were then being hotly debated and
explored) and earlier, late-medieval effects placing
bodies (and trees like the Baptism's) in a floating,
detached relationship with the scene. In Piero's
case, this often meant placing a protagonist (human or supra-human) over the perspectival vanishing point of the painting, creating a co-presence for
the viewer rather than inviting them into an illuso-
ry space of depth and containment.

The convergence of parallel lines in pictorial representation was known and shown from Roman
times, and is (obviously) one aspect of our everyday perception of rectilinear (urban or architectural) space. In Ancient Greece it was not used
in depictions, but the slight swelling of built columns (known as *entasis*), and the upwards bulging
of temple pediments (as at the Parthenon) were
thought to provide visual correction for the sagging
or deflation which were proper to straight, parallel
lines when perceived by the human eye.

Global View

Antique optics were based on spherical projection, which is actually closer to how the eye - as an orb-receives information on the retina than are the rigid lines of early Renaissance art. 15th-century architect Filippo Brunelleschi is credited with creating the method for capturing 'realistic' space in depth by faithfully copying the projection on a flat mirror plane of two scenes in his native Florence: the Duomo Baptistery (with a single vanishing point) and the Piazza della Signoria (with two points, left and right). Alberti theorized that the picture is a window derived as a slice through the eye's visual 'pyramid,' in other words, a flat plane which negates the actual curving properties of our retinal vision, and which is situated outside of the body, before our eyes. There is a double distancing, both world and projection being externalised, flattened and homogenised, perhaps analogous to Latour's 'globalised' world of infinite resource and extents, which we convince ourselves we can float above and through as a disembodied, disengaged eye, rather than acknowledging that we are in an intimate, physical, biological embrace with it. Outside versus Inside.

The art historian Erwin Panofsky wrote in his essay *Perspective as Symbolic Form* that

> [linear perspective] is as much a consolidation of the external world as an extension of the self...space is continuous...by nature, before all bodies and beyond all bodies, indifferently receiving everything.

Panofsky (1991)
p. 66

There was a significant theological motivation underlying the resurgence of perspective in the 15th century. According to Panofsky, it marked the end of antique theocracy and the beginning of a period (charged by the rediscovery of Greco-Roman art) in which the human became central, infused with divinity, perfectly proportioned: what he calls the *anthropocracy*. The vanishing point -where all parallel lines converge at the horizon- introduces a note of the infinite, the divine, into this otherwise human-centred optics. Man and God coexist on the same plane, the latter infusing the former, and not getting in his way, not blocking the view.

I would propose that *anthropocracy* is a forebear and progenitor of *Anthropocene*. If space is both 'indifferently receiving' and 'an extension of the self' (a newly-charged, egotistical - even narcissistic - notion of self), then it is easy to see how a powerful tool like perspective could lead us to feel that our visual rays - beaming out, mapping and organising the territory as it appears from our positions, projecting order onto inchoate space, rendering space both subjective and measurable - must resonate with the imperative of Genesis 1 (seen earlier) that man has God-granted (and, now, God-like) dominion over the world.

Death / Depth

All of which leads us back to Uccello's painting of a night hunt in a forest.

Uccello was deeply concerned with linear perspective and was a great innovator with the tool. Vasari recounts in his (sometimes gossipy) *Lives of the Artists* that Uccello's young wife once implored him to her bed whilst he was working late at night. 'Ah,' he responded, 'but perspective is so sweet.' It's not too much of a stretch to see him as a contemporary distracted lover, in thrall to a distant, screen-based partner. Uccello did not merely make use of perspective (as a pianist might of different scales); he folded it into his paintings as a leitmotif and a source of meaning. Perhaps whilst avoiding his

Vasari (2008) p. 41

103

lusty wife, he concocted extraordinary see-through visions of complex circular objects, such as the 2400 construction points of planes on a complex vase. His approach mirrors exactly that of computer graphics 500 years later, where realistic renderings are made up of countless facets, composed, manipulated and viewed by artists in the same 'wireframe' style prior to their fleshing-out with material and light. Drawn to circular objects such as toroidal or doughnut-shaped 'mazzochi' hats, Uccello placed them in vast and complex scenes (such as his celebrated battle triptych), showing the elementary, stable formation of pure shapes in a chaotic scene. In these cases, the mazzochi were almost always reduced to a low-def black and white patchwork of rectangular facets, showing the method more than the object.

The battle scenes (and in particular the best-preserved one, of San Romano, in London's National Gallery) are - amongst many other things - essays in the construction of space. The vertical middle ground is composed of assorted horses and humans jostling, filling up the picture plane with a massed energy of conflict. Beneath them, armour-wearing corpses and broken lances (the detritus of the battle above) are organised according to conventional perspective forms, pointing towards the vanishing point as if they were the lines on a calm urban pavement. The background landscape tilts upwards and fills the top half of the picture: there is no relief, no geometric escape from this scene of destruction.

The Night Hunt in the Forest clearly refers to elements of the battle paintings, with a similar group of men on horses bent on violence. In other respects it is a unique and troubling image. Housed in Oxford's Ashmolean Museum, it is big (165 by 65 cm) and therefore enveloping: as viewer, you can get lost in its depths. It may also be significant that it was Uccello's last recorded work, perhaps his final statement on a lifetime's reflection on depth and perception. Indeed, we might view it as being like Prospero's renunciation of his magic at the end of The Tempest, because Uccello shows us - more than anything else - the expiration of the human gaze when confronted with a forest. The disappearance of the vanishing point.

It so happened that my first direct encounter with this extraordinary painting coincided with a reunion (after thirty years) with a high school girlfriend from Los Angeles, who was in Oxford to visit her daughter and son in law. I scuttled to the Ashmolean ahead of this encounter, brimming with nerves, possessed with a heightened sense of the depth and circularity of time, worried about looking inwards towards my etiolated, long-haired 18 year-old self, who seemed to occupy me like a scaled-down ghost; as if my current, well-rounded persona was a self-satisfied suit of clothes over a diminished, departed, more urgent and more naive version of me. I spent two hours staring at the painting, and then returned the following day.

In the forest scene, there is no central tree à la Piero: there are four very similar foreground trees (identified by art historians as *quercus palustris*, or 'parasol oaks') which form three windows into the rest of the forest. The further trees are not planted on a grid (unlike the serried, sacrificial Douglas-Fir above my village in Burgundy): they are consonant (practically identical, in fact), but randomly arranged. They recede from view, reproducing into myriad quantities, stretching every way, eventually disappearing into an eerie darkness which may be a result of the depth and density of the forest, the darkness of the night, or a harbinger of death. They are all lopped, cut to allow the passage of the view (and the hunt). There is not one vanishing point,

despite the stable horizontal composition: there are thousands. The power of perspective to control and define space has been comprehensively erased by this dark forest.

The human and animal protagonists of the scene seem to respond rather more to this condition of disorientation than to the linear process of a hunt, tracing a vector, smelling blood, arriving by a line to a final point of destruction. Instead, dogs, horses and hunters on foot are running willy-nilly, racing in various directions. There is a general trend - towards the centre of the painting - but this is significantly undermined by many elements: a rider to the right whose horse has reared, as if afraid to cross the plane of a foreground tree; and - in particular - the greyhounds at the head of the chase, deeper inside, who are darting in every which way, totally confused about the course to follow.

The 13 horses and their riders and the 22 dogs differ in real, painted size from 15 centimetres to barely 1, according to their recession in the forest; however, they are all rendered in equal detail irrespective of depth or size. They cavort uniquely, all distinctly individual, showing off the crispness of their profiles in motion, arching stomachs, curving tails, springing legs all set apart from the gloomy background. The scene is nocturnal, but they are all evenly lit, as if emitting their own luminescence. The forest itself dissolves into darkness (but without atmosphere), and its human and animal actants disport themselves without hierarchy or seeming effect by the surroundings, other than a progressive geometric disappearance.

No being is master of this space, above all the viewer. Everything is equal in its expiring depths.

It's tempting to view this painting as showing the resignation of an elderly person, no longer in thrall to his methods and gifts, to the overpowering of space. At one with the world.

Everything is visible, nothing is clear.

My nerves dissipated instantly on reuniting with my old girlfriend. Our shells had changed, but our personhood was the same, just smudged out across decades of experience. It turned out that there was no reason for my apprehension before this time-capsule moment: upon opening, its depths contained merely the present. She brought some photos from the early days, including one of my parents' house as they first inhabited it (and when she visited). There was no lush, narrative, detailed garden cared for over decades by my father, but just a patch of lawn against a brick wall. And there, captured in time and two dimensions, standing at the edge of a rudimentary patio whose rectilinear concrete flagstones receded from view in one-point perspective, was a spindly pine in a pot, the youthful manifestation of the bonsai which outlived my father and which now graces my own small garden in Burgundy.

Leonardo's Shapeshifting Forest

I would like to contrast Uccello's magnificent vision with the furtive tree-thoughts of his compatriot, Leonardo da Vinci. Uccello was 55 when Leonardo was born; the younger man struggled to make definitive paintings as clear and complete as the *Night Hunt in the Forest*: he sometimes spent decades on an individual work, dragging them around on his frequent travels, alienating patrons who had paid for him to come up with the goods a long time before receiving (sometimes incomplete) masterpieces. He has left us only 15 paintings. It is hardly surprising that Leonardo was so shifty, so uncertain with these complete statements: he was obsessed from an early age with performing something essentially impossible, namely the capturing of movement and of the fugitive effects of air, wind, water, plants and bodies in a state of transience. His frowning, spread-eagled Vitruvian Man (encountered previously in our story) was perhaps the most notable exception, pinned like a butterfly to the picture plane, flattened out, showing -as a captive- his ideally-proportioned limbs in two positions on the same page.

Leonardo was apparently far more at home, far better adapted, to the evanescent, conditional form of his dozens of notebooks, which cover a vast range of subjects, usually in a fragmentary manner. It is of particular interest to us here that he was often concerned with the growth and form of trees. His great paintings (The Mona Lisa, the Virgin of the Rocks) show an intense interest in botany, tiny flowers and leaves rendered with as much care as the former's elusive smile. I encountered his notebooks en masse in the unprecedented and probably unique retrospective exhibition at the Louvre in 2020. Even in this choice of format he was rather fluid: the sizes are very varied, but share a surprisingly miniature quality. He probably had one or more of them on his person at all times, to record fleeting thoughts, ideas, inventions and effects.

He showed little care for 'proper' or balanced composition on the page, frequently crowding a scene into a tiny corner of an already tiny book. In the Institut de France Manuscript M there is an astonishing cluster of drawings in which he attempts to map the underlying structure of a tree as it grows out its branches. One sketch - only a centimeter or so across - shows a mature tree trunk and branches with the ghost form of its former self contained inside, exactly how I felt facing Uccello's painting, inhabited by another version of myself.

Leonardo was preoccupied with flux at different timescales, those of the growing tree being too slow to manifest to the watching eye, but nonetheless essential for understanding the final form. At the

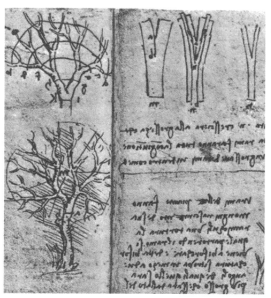

Leonardo da Vinci, growth of trees in the notebook in the Institut de France (1513)

other extreme of this temporal scale, he invented the swimming goggles so that he could observe under the waters of the Arno river the precise, swirling movement of bright metal flecks launched into the stream by an assistant. He left behind one very large (but little-known, and badly-damaged) work which registers this sense of immersion in time and movement, of surrender to the organic forces of a forest which envelops and exceeds human perception: a kind of installation-scale replica of the atmosphere of Uccello's Night Hunt, as if we were inside the painting.

The Sala delle Asse is a large, square, vaulted room in Milan's Sforzesco Castle. The Castle was the only built work of the early Renaissance architect Filarete, who we saw earlier depicting Adam as a biological self-builder, sheltering himself from the rain with a roof made of his hands as he was expelled from Paradise. The room's name may well be a misnomer, derived from a message about the hasty removal of scaffolding planks (*asse*) after Leonardo hurriedly completed his commission to decorate the room in 1498 (twenty-eight years after Uccello's hunt scene). The room is a painted forest, with gnarled roots emerging from rocks around the floor level, rising in spindly trunks which then knit together into a complete, convoluted tree canopy on the vaulted ceiling. At the apex the smaller branches knit together into a kind of wreath bearing the Sforza shield; there are specks of blue sky visible between the leaves.

Much of what we see today is corrupted, restored in opaque conditions in 1902 (some bright colours were almost certainly added in an unjustified interpretation; the restoring team did little to document the stages of their work). After a more faithful restoration in the 1950s, an even more painstaking, laser-scraping attempt was concluded in 2018.

Leonardo may have appreciated these fugitive metamorphoses: this forest has grown in ways its author did not intend, and we will probably never
find its 'original' state. Nevertheless, the lower-level
monochrome roots (some of which were protected by previous wooden paneling) are clearly by his
hand, and possess an impressive, dynamic power.
It does not take much to imagine these vines and
shoots growing visibly or shaking in the wind.

Notwithstanding these art-historical caveats, this
extraordinary work still speaks to us (perhaps more
so now than ever). It lacks human scale, hierarchy
and reference. The eye is bombarded, bewildered
with a mass of organic detail extending beyond the
visual field. We are invited to lose ourselves, to experience envelopment; to dwell - within the confines of a square room - in a non-geometric space
which is connected to a far greater environment
beyond.

In other words - those of Bruno Latour - Leonardo
invites us *to exist inside*, to experience (through artifice) our belonging to the terrestrial through an almost full-scale reproduction of the living structures
of the Critical Zone. He projects us towards empathy with the forest. He indicates that we can -and
should- be at home there, amongst the growth, the
movement, the fruitfulness, the sheer diversity and
the interconnectedness of everything.

Extant fresco by
Leonardo da Vinci,
Sala delle Asse.
Following page:
Wall and ceiling of
the Sala delle Asse

Donald Trump and the Hedges of Ulster

The Californian city named Paradise was scorched to the ground by a forest fire in November 2018. Donald Trump immediately visited with California Governor Jerry Brown - someone who is the absolute antithesis of the orange President, an acolyte of my radical, spiritual teacher Ivan Illich, and a gentle, thoughtful man. The horror of the situation - and the need for federal funds - made Brown swallow any possible personal disgust, and travel to survey the damage with his ideological nemesis. Trump was in character: expert in all matters, he offered some unsolicited advice to the suffering, expelled Paradisians, advice which contained - as it often does with him - both braggadocio and implicit criticism, pick-me-up and put-you-down. It turned out that Paradise had not been sufficiently raked. Trump blurted:

> I was with the president of Finland and he said: 'We have, much different, we are a forest nation.' He called it a forest nation. And they spend a lot of time on raking and cleaning and doing things, and they don't have any problem.

Cited in
The Guardian,
November 19th 2018

Finnish president Sauli Niinistö was surprised to find himself invoked in this way, as he had said no such thing - only that there was a wide network of monitoring of Finland's forests (which cover 75 per cent of the country). Perhaps - charitably - this can be included in Trump's awesomely vague 'doing things.' However, one pithy protesting placard

116

brandished at Trump on a subsequent visit perhaps summed up the situation best. 'We're in a drought, moron,' it read, which deflated his argument on two accounts: it rains a lot in Finland, making forest fires a rarity; and California was then - as it is at the time of writing - in the grip of a longstanding absence of precipitation. The understory brush was like tinder.

Forests have always been modified by fires, usually started by lightning. Periodic burning serves to create a tabula rasa, allowing the best-adapted species to regrow. Some trees (such as pines) are designed to seed during fires, their cones releasing their precious germs in response to heat. Humans of all stripes - as we shall see - have also used fire to adapt the forest to their needs, with widely differing effects. The only thing that doesn't appear to happen in forests is the original fire described by Vitruvius earlier in our story, in which branches rubbing together in the wind spontaneously combust, thereby generating human sociability (and language) around the bonfire, and then architecture.

In the case of California's Paradise-hell, the forest had ceased to be adapted to the prevailing climate conditions, conditions which - as we have seen - have been changed by humanity, with Trump as the apex-human, the climate crisis denier-in-chief at that time. His musings on wood have been repudiated in other circumstances: when the so-called 'forest' of millennial, massive timbers supporting Notre Dame's roof caught on fire (for reasons which are still unclear), Trump tweeted - as the drama was unfolding - that the French authorities should launch water-bombs from Canadair planes. No matter that the French fleet is based far south in Nîmes and requires open water to load up (not available in central Paris); the real glitch in his thinking was - again - related to fire-control method. Paris fire chief Lieutenant-Colonel Michael Bernier responded in real time (through Agence France Press), saying that releasing just one load from a Canadair

> with the equivalent of three tonnes of concrete dropped at 250 kilometres per hour .. would have been like bowling with the cathedral...the two towers might have fallen... Neighbouring buildings would have been hit by flying blocks of hot stone. It was technically impossible, undoable and most of all would have been utterly useless.

Quoted in Le Point, April 16th 2019

Ouch!

Trump's approximations are perhaps easier to understand when we consider that his landscapes of predilection require both extremely careful raking and dosing with vast quantities of water. His 17 golf courses are - in a way - a kind of anti-forest, vast clearings voided of any arboreal obstacles (except very carefully planned artificial ones), maintained in a state of improbable Edenic perfection and homogeneity by the illiberal use of irrigation and selective herbicides. They are rather like the airstrips and play-battlefields maintained by my father in cold war Germany, non-places, no-heres, groundless grounds. Organic processes and animated entities which might dare the slightest incursion into their single overriding purpose are immediately annihilated with intensive labour and poisonous chemicals.

Golf courses are inherently exclusive and damaging. Their core identity incarnates the desire of mostly rich, older white men to occupy vast areas of outdoor space in near solitude, without needing to fear the imperfections and energies of the natural world: no mud, no critters, no unexpected visitors.

118

The private outdoors. On the maps we saw generated for *Terra Forma* by multiple non-human inhabitants of the land, golf courses must show up like terra incognita, as forbidden as military ranges, animal no-go. The advocacy group Tourism Concern estimates that a typical tropical golf club annually requires a ton and a half of powerful fertiliser and pesticide, and consumes the fresh water resources of 60,000 villagers. [note: source] In the USA there are 16,000 golf courses, increasingly in the low-precipitation, high-retirement 'sunbelt' states. 28 of the 100 biggest freshwater consumers in the desert context of Las Vegas are golf courses. And it should go without saying that the incinerated Paradise, CA, boasted about 10 golf clubs in its environs.

When in the somewhat stabilising hands of his speechwriters, Trump has more carefully contrib-

Donald Trump on the site of his hoped-for Balmeenie golf course in Aberdeenshire, 2011 (PA Images)

119

uted to the peculiarly North American myth of the land, a myth which has nourished the 'perfection' delusions of the golf course; this is where it gets interesting - and fundamental - for our story. At the 2020 Republican National Convention, accepting his party's nomination to run again for the Presidency, Donald Trump invoked a smorgasbord of frontierspeople to give heft to his vision of the USA as a nation of plucky, domineering terraformers. He trumpeted:

> Our American ancestors sailed across the perilous ocean to build a new life on a new continent. They braved the freezing winters, crossed the raging rivers, scaled the rocky peaks, trekked the dangerous forests, and worked from dawn till dusk. These pioneers didn't have money. They didn't have fame. But they had each other. They loved their families, they loved their country, and they loved their God. When opportunity beckoned, they picked up their bibles, packed up their belongings, climbed into their covered wagons, and set out West for the next adventure. Ranchers and miners, cowboys and sheriffs, farmers and settlers. They pressed on past the Mississippi to stake a claim in the wild frontier. Legends were born. Wyatt Earp, Annie Oakley, Davy Crockett, and Buffalo Bill. Americans built their beautiful homesteads on the open range. Soon, they had churches and communities, then towns, and with time, great centers of industry and commerce.

Trump's skilful speech writers doubtless included this as a dog-whistle to suburban Americans ensconced in their self-conceptualised 'beautiful homesteads on the open range.' As a demographic Trump needed to convince, his campaign explic-

itly excited white non-city dwellers, who were en-
couraged to perceive themselves and their reclusive
'homesteads' as threatened by unruly and anguished
protestors, many of them African-American. Or
- let's say - generically restless brown people: the
heroism of the pioneers involved clearing both forests and their native inhabitants in order to create
such lovely 'open ranges.' Sharing the convention
podium with Trump were Mark and Patricia Mc-
Closkey from Saint Louis, Missouri, who famously
brandished arms against a group of black protestors
walking down their private street on the way to the
mayor's residence. (No prizes for guessing that the
McCloskeys' McMansion is situated a short drive
from the Highlands Golf and Tennis club.)

Frontier hokum

Beyond their toxic winking and whistling, Trump's
frontierspeople references are entirely hokum.
'Buffalo' Bill Cody and his sharpshooting sidekick
Annie Oakley were rather Trumpian reality-theatre stars for far longer than they actually worked
on anything resembling the frontier. Cody had a
brief career during the Civil War as a fast-riding
scout, an assassin of Indians, and then as a brutally
effective commercial buffalo hunter (he purport-
edly shot 4,282 of the beasts in eighteen months
- or eight a day, without a Sunday break). Oakley
- oddly, for someone of Quaker stock - took up
arms as a way out of grinding rural poverty and
abuse. Aged 25, she became a star attraction in
Cody's Wild West Show, dazzling audiences with
her marksmanship. Cody was known for embroi-
dering his past achievements and thereby building
his own myth - a form of currency in his roving
reality-theatre extravaganza, which was successful
for 34 years. Their spectacle forged in the public
mind throughout America and Europe a particular
image of the US frontier as a locus of daring, full of

exotic animals and exotic humans (many of whom - including Chief Sitting Bull - joined the show). By a rather odd coincidence, their constant touring took them to Hardelot in Northern France, which we will visit in the next section of this book as the site of a very quiet, earth-loving, wooden theatre I built in 2016.

If the frontier in our minds is -to a large extent- a simulacrum, a narrative as authentic as professional wrestling, as Trump's 'Apprentice' TV show, or as a suburban golf course 'landscape,' there is one name in this cast of characters who stands out from the crowd as something approaching the real deal, a veritable terraformer and a scion of the forest-clearing culture which germinated in Ulster in the 17th century. Let's tell the tall tale of Davey Crockett, King of the Wild Frontier.

We should start at the end and work backwards. Crockett (ancestral name Crocketagne, of French Huguenot extraction) sealed his legend by dying

Contemporary publicity from Buffalo Bill's circus (bnf)

'Buffalo' Bill Cody
and Chief Sitting Bull
(Library of Congress)

at the siege of the Alamo in 1835, defending the expansion onto Spanish-held terrain of the germinating United States. He had migrated to the contested territory of Texas (to claim some land through mercenary actions) after losing his seat in the House of Representatives. He had lost (in part) because he opposed Andrew Jackson's alarmingly popular and frankly-entitled *Indian Removal Act*. Despite Cody's support (as a lawmaker) of native rights, he had actively fought the Creek Indians as part of the Tennessee Militia. Indeed, during his upbringing in desperate poverty, migration and servitude, buffeted by natural disasters, parts of his family were captured and killed by Indians. The thrust of his life would involve attempting to secure the footholds of pioneer families in the judicially, socially and naturally chaotic and hostile conditions of the young Republic.

Crockett's family had been pushed around for prior generations, expelled from France as protestants, settling - along with many other key originary figures in America - in Ulster Province in the late 17th century. The migration in the 1700s of 250,000 protestants (mostly Presbyterians) from Ulster to the USA was fundamental for the future identity of the country which is still bolstered and fortified by its frontier mythology, as regurgitated by Donald Trump. The story is of interest to us because the tabula rasa attitude to the forest of Ulster was applied at the scale of a continent, and is still alive as an ideal of conquest, taken up in Brazil, Indonesia and parts of Africa, in a heady brew of fundamentalist religiosity and purist capitalism.

The Scots Irish are - now - a peculiar American ethnic group, hiding so much in plain sight as to be both invisible and all-pervasive. They are so marbled and dissolved through American life that they don't need an epithet or acronym: no Indian- African- Irish- Asian- or WASP prefix is required. They are merely - and completely - American. They count more than a third of US Presidents from amongst their ranks, including (Indian-removing) Jackson, Grant, Teddy Roosevelt, Wilson, Truman, Johnson, Nixon, Bush-Bush, Clinton and even Obama (on his mother's side). This is an extraordinary achievement when we consider that they were one tiny ethnic subgroup, who were sent from Scotland to Ireland by Elizabeth I and James I in order to help secure Ulster as a British Colony. The process was so brutal (on both sides, coloniser and colonised) that they could have disappeared without trace. The American frontier myth was forged in this trauma, then exported and enlarged.

The Hedges of Ulster

Ulster was - in the early 17th century - very heavily wooded. Derry's name means oak grove ('Doire' in modern Irish); there were, in fact, hardly any towns, the whole landscape used for itinerant farming. The colonisers at first thought that the natives were nomadic; they were, however, imperceptible, on the move, scattered, deeply rooted in the region's forests and bogs, living in small clusters of cottages at the scale of hamlets. A contemporary observer (using reductive ethnic shorthand) wrote:

> A squirrel might have hopped from tree to tree the whole way from Florence Court to Betulbert…the forest is so wild as to be scarce inhabited by any human creatures but ye O's and ye Mac's.

Bardon, 2012, p. 67

This posed a challenge for the colonisers: the land needed to be controlled, marshalled, transformed. What would soon be known as the Ulster Plantation had an Orwellian tinge to the name: the 'plants' (arable crops) only existed because other plants (trees) had been razed. The native Catholic Irish were as dissipated into this context as the Scots Irish would later be in United States society. As such they posed a serious threat, and had the upper hand in many early skirmishes as they could appear from the forest with surprise, and then vanish back into it. The answer to this invisibility was the axe; just as would be Agent Orange in the Vietnam War under (Scots Irish) Lyndon Johnson. The tabula rasa went as far as the creation of mini-hedges throughout the Ulster Plantation, the idea being that you could take a knee to shoot game (or perhaps a native) without affecting your line of sight. These shorter hedges distinguish to this day - biopolitically - landscapes of traditionally Protestant dominance from the flourishing, unruly hedges of Catholic areas. Paolo Uccello's dogs and hunters would have experienced no disorientation in such a landscape, the quarry picked out against a savagely cleared backdrop rather than lost in the depths of his dark, allegorical forest. This hunt was neither sport nor combat: it was an arboreal bloodbath, a genocide and an ecocide working hand-in-hand.

The Exported Ulster Frontier

Anthropologist William Cronon has beautifully documented the effects of these people - as settlers - on the northeastern US landscape in his book *Changes in the Land: Indians, Colonists and the Ecology of New England*. Like Ulster, the 'New' England was quite literally uncharted in the 1600s: the early maps showed only the line of the coast, the juncture of sea and undifferentiated, unfathomable territory. Early visitors were most impressed by the abundance of this coastscape: brackish rivers choked with salmon, flocks of birds so vast that they would darken the sky as they flew over, huge stands of multi-centennial pine trees. The Scots Irish migrated in an unbroken wave, whose greatest intensity was from 1717 to 1770. Sent to sort out the natives in Ireland, they fell from favour and were persecuted under Charles I. So they moved on and applied the same methods elsewhere.

The New England Forest - blank on the maps - was, in reality, a richly-negotiated co-habitat of human, vegetal and animal. The Indians - like the Irish - lived in villages, in the former case easily demountable for seasonal movement (besides the well-known triangular teepee, they also mastered demountable wood frame construction). The womenfolk transformed the bounty and raised the young within the stockade; the men ranged afar, modifying the forest to optimise both game hunting and arable yields. They practiced selective burning and cutting in order to develop differing densities. One type of thicket known as 'abode of owls' was created to gather prey before flushing it into adjacent open territory for capture and culling. There was abundant agroforestry, maize grown in clearings, permaculture and careful rotation practiced so as to optimise and secure long-term yields. The liminal condition between forest and clearing was stretched and wiggled as much as possible in order to maximise the available areas of transit (and therefore hunting). The forest was an artifice, but it was built of its own best characteristics, never mutated against its nature. Existing gradients of density (around rivers and wetlands) were used as the basis of what Cronon calls the 'mosaic' pattern which characterised Indian forest husbandry.

The early settlers, Trump's plucky Bible-lugging pioneers, were almost wiped out by their own ignorance of the land. Half of the first pilgrims in Plymouth died within a year. This was as much through ineffective farming as through an inability to adapt to new pathogens. The microbial mat mentioned at the beginning of this book on the northeastern US seaboard contained bacteria too unfamiliar for Calvinist and Scots Ulster immune systems. At the same time, the sheer bountifulness went to people's heads: settler William Wood recounts oysters a foot long and game fowl so dense that fifty could be killed with a single shot.

The same went for the forest. England had restrictions in force on cutting timber since 1543 as the land had essentially been deforested. This was problematic: naval supremacy depended on a ready supply of old-growth pines - measuring up to a hundred metres - for strong, single-element masts. Ancient forests were plundered without any notion of balance or resilience: when a large tree was cut for warlike needs, the practice of 'driving a piece' was often used, consisting of sacrificing many smaller trees to block the fall of a larger one, preventing splintering or shattering. Wood was shipped back on wooden ships: when the Fortune was first sent back to England from the American colonies in 1621, its cargo consisted of three barrels of furs, the entirety of the remaining payload being

Micihgan loggers at work, 1890 (Alamy)

timber. In the new colonies, 80 per cent of wood was used for fuel.

The harsh climate of New England - with hot, humid summers and freezing winters lasting sometimes six months - was thought to be bio-modifiable through the eradication of trees. This contrary, numbskull idea - worthy of Trump's water-dumping suggestion on Notre Dame - was even promoted by Jefferson and Benjamin Franklin, who wrote that 'cleared land absorbs more heat and melts snow faster.' Such thinking, as well as the profitability of potash (made from simply burning forests), and the demand for white oak in the Caribbean (to fill ships with barrelled rum for the return journey to Europe once they had been voided of the cargo of slaves) meant that anxious settlers saw deforestation as a sure thing, an easy buck. Indians even got in on the act, using their axe skills to make wood shingles for export back to their colonisers' homeland.

From a letter in 1793, quoted in Buck (2017)

Top: Bannock family
uses young saplings
to support their
teepee
(Alamy)

Bottom: Engraving by
W H Bartlett of a US
pioneer settlement in a
partially-cleared forest
(Alamy)

Alongside this, it was common for settlers to boast to freezing Old-Englanders that they had open hearths in every room, log fires crackling without constraint. (Their German-ancestry neighbours had imported far more efficient closed stoves).

Of course it couldn't last. The push westwards, despoiling ever vaster Indian lands, legally sanctioned by horrors such as Jackson's Indian Removal Act, was an effect of the rapid exhausting of the Northeastern forests. As in Old England, once cut down (at the rate of an acre per year for heating a single house), forests would not grow back at the required pace. The valuable giant pines and cedars would take centuries to regrow, and they would remain contested right through to the 20th century, their few remaining oldest cousins becoming - in their 1990s death-throes - the protagonists of Richard Powers' mighty tree-novel *The Overstory*.

The North American Indians were not entirely the sensitive eco-warriors of contemporary legend: they modified the forest continuously, but were not so populous (nor so reckless) as to exhaust it in the way the colonists did, cranking up the heat like there's no tomorrow (something echoed - centuries later - by Trump's over-consuming, shag-pile, overblown, aircon open-range suburbanites). Further south at the same time, the Spanish genocide of South American Indians was producing a paradoxical effect: their decimation, being so vast, had the effect of creating a measurable uptick in atmospheric oxygen at a planetary scale. They had lived - in such great numbers - much like the forest-bending Indians of New England, and the canopy recovered entirely when they were gone. The ice caps, drilled out in cores to reveal the air-story of the world, noted this sad fact, and the date of 1610 is held by some to mark the beginning of the Anthropocene, the fully-fledged anthropocracy of the planet and its soils, air, rocks and water. Further afield, on Easter Island, natives had razed the surface of trees. And in New Zealand the Maori had destroyed half the islands' forest in less than 50 years from 900 AD.

See 'Defining the Anthropocene,' Simon Lewis, Mark Maslin, Nature 519 (2015)

Our story of wilful dominance over the arboreal world - sanctioned by our interpretations of the Old Testament - started in earnest in the time of Shakespeare. Historians normally date the Industrial Revolution as the beginning of our serious impact on the world, through the extensive burning of coal. But we only turned to coal - in places like the Forest of Dean - because we had killed the trees (and let's not forget that coal is merely compressed, fossilised trees). The Ulster Plantation and its after-effects are, in fact, the antechamber of our current desolation, their motivating ideas and forces still alive and well. And coming out of the mouths of global political leaders.

The Thinking Forest (Mongongo Leaf)

Now we will examine what rather different things happen when humans live continuously - and without being disturbed - in the forest.

In the tropical belt of our planet the forests have been inhabited continuously for many thousands of years. Hidden in the semi-darkness under a canopy of palms, dispersed tribal groups still live in the manner of their furthest ancestors, who could be our Mesolithic cousins who dug barrows and made stone circles in the landscape surrounding my father's house, leaving the earliest traces on the maps with which we began this section of our story.

We - advanced, 'modern' westerners - have failed to show any respectful interest in our contemporaneous forest-dwellers until only about 70 years ago. I propose to look at three examples of in-depth encounters, spanning in time from one of the first studies to a recent account, and travelling in space from Central Africa to Ecuador and Brazil. The Frankenstein assemblage of Ascension Island sits - geographically - skewered by the equator, somewhere in the middle of all this.

The Mbuti

Pioneering anthropologist Colin Turnbull was the first westerner to carry out - in 1951 - extensive (and empathetic) fieldwork with forest-dwelling pygmies in Central Africa. He lived among the Mbuti people in the Ituri forest in (modern-day) Democratic Republic of Congo for two extended periods, learning their language, sharing their home conditions, following them as they hunted, mourned, celebrated and engaged (somewhat) with the outside world. His book *The Forest People* is a classic work of popular anthropology, and an extraordinary insight into a society utterly at odds with our own in that it was (and is) based entirely around the celebration of and cooperation with their verdant, bounteous habitat. Turnbull followed up with *The Mountain People*, which recounts the death-throes of The Ik tribe as they are forced off their habitual lands by nation-state border changes. Theatre director Peter Brook (who we shall meet in the next part of this book) made *The Ik* (in 1975) into a seminal performance about the limits of cooperation between humans and a landscape. Taken as paired projects, Turnbull's books are premonitory of the painful social collapse which ensues when a human group is no longer able to subsist from its habitual 'footprint.' Our societies are far more complex and far-reaching in their supply chains than those of the Ik or Mbuti, but the effect remains the same. We would do well - as Bruno Latour insistently advocated - to consider exactly what we depend on - as individuals - before making sweeping proposals for change at a planetary scale. (This book is - in some ways - is an attempt to do exactly that.) Everything is related, woven and webbed together, and we need to know what happens when we cut (or pull) a particular thread. Turnbull's Forest and Mountain People are deeply instructive - at their particular scales - in understanding how this web works, what animates it.

If the Mbuti escaped documentation for so long, it is partly because they were hidden from view (not unlike Ulster's 'ye O's and ye Macs' in the preceding section). As Turnbull says: 'you can't find the Mbuti; they have to find you.' He was found by chance, not intending to study them on his first trip. The

Mbuti live in a degree of symbiosis with settled, agrarian, village-dwelling communities; they share food and resources, some ceremonies, superficial social ties, and weapons (especially metal spears for hunting elephants). Turnbull encountered them as they had emerged into this village clearing; the Mbuti, however, were of no fixed abode, changing camp once a month or so to improve their chances at hunting forest game, and so as not to exhaust natural supplies of berries, mushrooms, honey and roots. Their fundamental, unchanging abode, their locus, background, reciprocal collective being (and source of wonder) is the forest itself. Turnbull describes their extraordinary oneness with this context, their profound skill at reading processes of growth and vegetal collaboration, their capacity to move silently and at great speed so as not to alert predators such as leopards. He also recounts how they relate philosophically to this all-providing milieu.

They live in collectives of five or six families in hamlet-scaled groups which do not fundamentally transform the forest. They are very far from Viollet-le-Duc's disparaged, dirty, ignorant savages, needing a civilisational bricolage helping-hand from a time-travelling Frenchman in order to finish their hut. Mbuti settlements are a thing of wonder, made in response to their high-speed trans-forest lifestyle. When the decision is made to move on (by the best hunters, the only, default and non-elected 'leaders' in their society) the whole group speeds through the forest to a new location and the family dwellings are then made in less than a day by the women. And they are architecturally extraordinary, nothing like the ponderous tectonics of Vitruvius' temple-hut or Viollet-le-Duc's self-aggrandising gothic cone. In fact, they were rediscovered in the later 20th century as ideally efficient shelters by visionary architect Buckminster Fuller. They are framed geodesic domes, perhaps thousands of years old in their conception. Turnbull watches one builder:

> She squatted down making her own home, driving the saplings into the ground with sharp thrusts each time in exactly the same place. When she had completed a circle she stood up and deftly bent the *fito* [poles] over her head, twisting them together and twining smaller saplings across forming a lattice framework. When she had finished, she took the [Mongongo] leaves we had collected and slit the stalks towards the end, like clothes pegs, hooking two or three of them together. When she had enough she started hanging them like tiles on the framework, overlapping each other and forming a waterproof covering. Turnbull 2015 p. 62

The saplings and Mongongo are abundant, so there is no need to discriminate for a location, or to transport materials from afar. The camp would bring their sparse belongings wrapped up in leaves and - most importantly - smouldering logs, which they would periodically stop to relight with kindling. The Mbuti are capable of many things, but making fire from scratch is not one of them. As fire is fundamental for heating and drying out huts, for smoking meat and scaring off predators at night, it became perhaps the greatest treasure to be transported - like the Olympic torch - in their mad dashes from one camp to a new one.

Women tended to remain at camp, looking after children and keeping food on the go, whilst the men went and hunted and bartered. It is - I think - significant that the women should be the continuity, the repository of knowledge, as well as the ex-

Mbuti woman building
her village, 2005
(Randy Olson)

pert crafting hands of the Mbuti's buildings. Whilst there is some strict gender separation for certain ceremonies (including the Molimo, which we shall shortly describe), Turnbull notes that the BaMbuti society is -in practice- free of hierarchy. Everyone is free to mock anyone (there is a great deal of laughter), there are fights, but they are carried out in a manner as if a good outcome was always to be expected. Things are not serious, because they have faith in their milieu and in their destiny; their relaxed attitude breeds a slightly anarchic mood, where the absence of rules allows a trusting, jostling negotiation of myriad situations. They are fundamentally happy.

By the same token, there is no overarching mythological structure to their thoughts and beliefs; they are as laid back and formless as a Japanese Shinto's, as we shall see in the next section of this book. If there is anything resembling a deity in their society, it is a very practical and intimate one -the forest itself. Turnbull describes how the BaMbuti have an attitude towards degrees of death, the worst (and most irreversible) being 'completely dead.' The village having accompanied the elderly Balemakito through the initial stages of being dead, her 'complete' death provokes pandemonium, and an assiduous effort to make sense of it. There is violent mourning, wailing, convulsions as people fight to get into her hut to see her. The menfolk decide that these exceptional circumstances require a three month-long deployment of the *Molimo*. The term itself is shifty, and the 'ceremony' (in reality, a bit more like a music festival) is open-ended, not strictly defined. It is more mood than ritual, and certainly not perceived as invoking the supernatural; this is hardly necessary as the Mbuti see the forest itself as so animated as to be a kind of systemic deity, present and enveloping, all-providing.

The Molimo takes places every evening after dinner during the mourning period, the women (on this rare occasion) banished to their huts. 'Molimo' is described as 'the great animal of the forest.' A growling, howling sound emerges from the trees around the camp, plaintive, deep and distant, moving around. It could be partly animal, perhaps a leopard, but there is an other-worldly character to the sound (it should be said that the forest is a constant immersive soundscape, with interjections in three dimensions from birds, monkeys and - according to the tribespeople - the plangent chameleon). In reality the Molimo sounds are made by a disguised member of the tribe vocalising into a length of drainpipe, something which everyone probably knows; but the sounds allow them to suspend disbelief and be transported.

The men cannot be passive to this forest emanation: they must sing back to it. Their music - improvised for hours on end, consisting of peals of polyrhythmic notes accompanied by some gentle percussion - has one purpose: to sing back to the external Molimo their appreciation of the forest. They are also gently exhorting it to 'wake up' (something the Japanese still do as a matter of daily habit - through clapping - to Shinto deities). Their gentle, rolling chorus - as recorded by Turnbull - deeply inspired pioneering jazz drummer Elvin Jones, and was folded into the John Coltrane Quartet's quests for a universal sound. Re-awakening the forest is done in the hope that - in future - everything will come right, tragic events such as Balemakito's death being the exception rather than the rule. Turnbull cites Moke to this effect:

> When something big goes wrong…it must be because the forest is sleeping and not looking after its children. So what do we do?

We wake it up. We wake it up by singing
to it, and we do this because we want it to
awaken happy.

The Molimo is a performance in which there is no
particular hierarchy, no sky-gods being begged for
bountifulness; it *enacts* rather than representing or
repeating a state of being which is acknowledged to
be fundamentally beneficent, although in need of
occasional maintenance. The Mbuti see themselves
as indissociable from the forest, which shelters them
and provides (almost) everything they need.

After this extended Molimo, it was felt that justice
had been done to the poor Balemikato. The camp
then moved on, restarting the life-process with the
forest over again.

This is a snapshot of a particular moment in the
Mbuti's lives. It could date from yesterday or several hundred years ago; they have no notion of
history, apart from the memory of their immediate ancestors: they have no Yggdrasil, no banyan of enlightenment, no errant cross to which
everything refers and defers. They live in the hy-
per-intense present of forest time. The present of
the outside has - very sadly - made incursions into
their world in recent years, with malevolent politicians - such as Jean-Pierre Bemba in the Democratic Republic of Congo - leading bloodthirsty
quests to 'erase the blackboard' of the pygmies'
world. There is not necessarily even a financial angle to such raids, merely the fear of the void and of
difference. There are rumours of cannibalism, of
pygmy flesh being somehow magical. Thousands
have been killed, but tens of thousands remain,
invisible in the forest.

The Achuar

French anthropologist Philippe Descola followed
Turnbull's path into the forest a couple of decades
later, to encounter - during a continuous three-year
residence - the Achuar people, living in the Ama-
zonian rainforest in Ecuador, near the border with
Peru. As with Turnbull, the empathetic depth of
his encounter would not only sweep away earlier
studies depicting the Achuar rather simplistically as
colourful, exotic and warlike, but would also add
a new (and distinctive) building-block onto the
theories of Descola's master, Claude Lévi-Strauss.
Descola's distinctive insight would concern how
humans can relate to forest nature *per se*, as 'social
partners,' rather than as the ground for projections
of our own relations.

The Achuar are a subdivision of the (then)
100,000-strong Jivaro tribe (Jivaro being a Spanish
adaptation of their own name, the Shiviar). Descola's immersion and discipline allowed a new and
nuanced portrait of his subjects to take shape. Like
the Mbuti, they live in a relatively well-adapted and
harmonious relation with the forest and its various
animal inhabitants. Having measured their calorie
intake (previously thought to be inadequate), Descola discovered that they were - in fact - living ful-
ly and very lightly, exploiting their context to only
about 30 per cent of its capacity. They worked on
average 3 hours a day in order to subsist. Turnbull
had earlier contrasted the Mbuti's leisurely lifestyle
with that of the agricultural villagers with whom
they lived in some symbiosis: the Mbuti would take
what they needed from the forest, the villagers having to toil endlessly and against pests and diseases
in order to produce enough food. This relative ease
left both tribes plenty of time in which to think,
discuss and praise their host context.

Unlike the Mbuti, the Achuar exploited agricultural plants, but they did so in a way which did not entail severe distinction. They would burn a clearing, using the tree ash to fertilise the land, and would plant up to 60 varieties of plants whose own interdependence and symbiosis had been learned for generations. Their 'gardens' were in fact structured a lot like the surrounding forest, unruly, vertically mixed. They were guided in their dreams by Shakain, the (male) forest spirit, who would indicate to them the most propitious pieces of the forest for a new garden. These gardens were - whilst managed separately - seen as being *of the forest*, and were allowed to return to a free condition after 3 or 4 years' exploitation. Descola noted that the returning forest was often denser and healthier in these ex-gardens.

The whole of Amazonia - 6 million square kilometres stretching to the south of Brazil, inhabited by countless tribes with over 400 principal language groups - has been used in this way (or similar ways) by humans for perhaps 8,000 years. There is no 'primal' forest, everything is a result of intervention, exploitation, return. The forest exists in a perpetual present which is the result of a continuous collaboration between humans, animals and plants.

Unlike the Mbuti, the Achuar reside in stable settlements, in large, wooden collective houses which would contain several polygamous groupings: perhaps ten adults, and as many as twenty-five children. The group would gather each day around a fire before dawn and recount their dreams collectively. These were parsed for signs of how better to live with the forest. Interpretation was metaphorical rather than direct, an animal standing in for a person, a glass necklace seen as representing an omen of animal entrails in a successful hunt. A dreamer self-conceived as a disembodied spirit, able to trav-

144

el outside of the body to meet other spirits with human attributes of speech, who would represent both animals and plants. The dreams would lead to the chanting of Anent, highly-codified songs addressed to spirits such as Nunkui, the (female) guardian of the Achuar gardens. The spirits of the cultivated plants were conceptualised as blood relations to the dreamer, animal spirits as in-laws and more distant relations. The communal dream structure would allow reception of the ideas and desires of the 'social partner' plants and animals regarding the best manner to execute their destiny as a shared endeavour with humans.

These rich and lengthy observations led Descola to break from the 'totemic' model of Lévi-Strauss, which consisted of mapping parallels in human relations onto the non-human world: so-and-so would be seen as an eagle whereas another would be like a bear, not because of the relations between bear and eagle, but because of a mapping of human characteristics onto non-human entities. For the Achuar - and thus for their observer Descola - there is a 'shared interiority' between human and non-human, plants able to speak to us as somehow-equals in our dreams, and conceived of as networked partners in waking life (hunted animals are considered kindred spirits worthy of compassion and honour). Decsola revivified the maligned and dusty term 'animism' in order to categorise this way of relating to the greater world, a term which has reentered general use as depicting life-systems which are receptive to the invisible world. We shall see it later, alive and well, in ultra-modern contemporary Japan. And I will appropriate it at the end of this book in relation to the death of a kindred spirit in my family.

The Thinking Forest

Another generation of anthropologists down the road, the Canadian Eduardo Kohn - working geographically alongside Descola in Upper Ecuador- extends the notion of animism to a more universalised view of the forest as a self-regulating, self-propelling, animated and living complex system possessing great and rich agency. In this respect it resembles Lovelock's Gaia, especially as seen by Bruno Latour as a self-conscious, self-propelling 'moment.'

Kohn - like his forebears - put in the empathic legwork, living with the Runa for four years, and returning regularly over a twenty-year period. The Runa have had to engage with external forces much more comprehensively than the Mbuti and Achuar, fighting Spanish colonists off (propelled to do so by their own dream-visions), and then entering a complex interdependence with them, hunting for them, weaving their western dress and hierarchical structures into their dream-worlds and waking attitudes. Kohn extends his insight from living alongside them to propose that it is entirely inadequate to view the human inhabitants of the forest in isolation, as somehow exceptional compared to other 'selves.' He relates how non-human agents in their forest - such as jaguars, the biggest predator besides the Runa - are seen as capable of thought, interpreting signs and symbols, to such an extent that they are taken into consideration as constituents in a much bigger system of common reflection extending far beyond the human. Dogs - who hunt with the Runa - are treated as autonomous beings, cohabiting with humans but responsible for their own upkeep. There are elaborate initiation rites (involving hallucinogens) to bring the dogs into a parallel-living in which they are not merely subservient, and have to occupy their own status. These ceremonies serve to instruct them in the moral code which they will have to follow - correct behaviour towards humans, dutifulness for hunting - in order to maintain their place in the web of relations particular to the rain forest context.

Kohn's point - expounded in his marvellous book 'How Forests Think' - is that we are only 'part of the flourishing,' that ''we' are not the only 'we'' in this forest, and that, as a result of this realisation, we might become 'less disjointed from the effects we have on the world.' The forest -as the locus and totality of these selves, human, animal, vegetal- is charged with its own particular system of thinking. One of the difficulties of this view is that we have to avoid projecting our own thoughts onto it and -in Kohn's terms learn to think 'with' and not just 'about' it.

From a lecture to Harvard University School of Divinity, January 8th 2018

This rapid trot through vast thickets of contemporary social science should not obscure from our view - with its jaunty pace - the fact that these radiant examples of humans living not just 'in harmony' with the forest as resource, but also as its happy, enlightened, inspiring, fulfilled co-subjects, are deeply threatened. They are threatened by economic forces, by changes in climate, and - today - by their vulnerability to pandemics. In Brazil in particular, the drive to convert sylvan habitats, produced by millennia of balanced coexistence, the will to raze - in order to plant profitable crops or to graze beef cattle for export, which will denude the soil in a short time - is fired up by the evangelism used by politicians such as Jair Bolsonaro as a base.

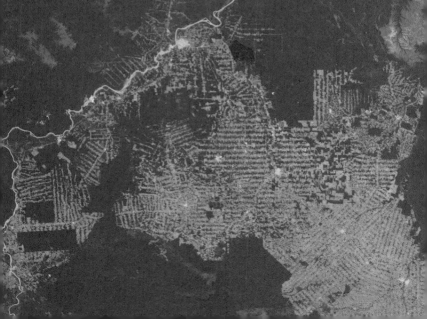

three

the
clearing

'It is only by recognising that all living things, whatever their specie, live a sole and same life, that a planetary and ecological politics can be founded. It is only when we recognise that the life that animates and traverses us is the same that animates and traverses a dandelion, a bird of paradise, but also mushrooms, bacteria and virus….that we can change our regard, our attitude and our actions towards the planet.'

Emanuele Coccia, interview in
Le Monde, August 5th 2020

Amazonia deforestation,
Rondônia, between 2002
(top) and 2012 (bottom)
Images: NASA/Landsat

The world is - according to philosopher Emanuele Coccia - an endless system of self-devouring, of a single life existing in a closed circuit, reliant - through plants - on the energy of the sun. In this single life of consumption and return, we are all making clearings around ourselves, constantly, and then allowing them to fill in - or actually feeding them - when we die. We hear a great deal today about limits, about how much we can reasonably devour (and how much less this will have to be in future). I want to end the arc of this book by suggesting that *how* we consume matters as much as *how much*: if we extract, kill and digest knowingly, mindfully, whilst respecting, acknowledging and - to a reasonable extent - *adapting to* the consumed entity, there is perhaps a chance that we will arrive at a balance of *quantities* through attention to *qualities*. I want to tell four stories to illustrate this, intimately in my own childhood, and reaching as far away and as (apparently) unfamiliar as can be, in animist Japan.

Road Tattoo
(Douglas-Fir)

A few years ago a curious graffito appeared on the road running through the centre of our village in Burgundy: in small cursive script in fine white spray paint, it comprised the word 'eiffage' adorned with a curving arrow pointing towards the road leading uphill to the east. Further inspection revealed a trail of the same nature terminating at the col in a ridge which overlooks the valley of the Saone, the Jura and - in clear conditions - Mont Blanc and the Western Alps.

Eiffage is a French construction conglomerate whose name tells a story. Turning over 14 billion euros in 2015, it became the fifth largest group in Europe after a merger in 1993 with two other giants, Fougerolle and SAE, collectively responsible for mega-projects such as the Louvre Pyramid, Frank Gehry's Vuitton Foundation and Norman Foster's Millau viaduct. Its name is a wink: specialised in metal construction and tracing its corporate history back to the 19th century, the original corporate division had borne the name of Gustave Eiffel until 2006 when this was prevented in a court judgement (the company still claims the famous tower as one of its creations). Eiffel himself had forbidden the use of his name following the imbroglio of the Panama Canal construction, in which he was (unjustly) dragged into a corruption scandal; he retired and reduced his personal identification only to his eponymous tower and the pioneering wind tunnel and aerodynamic research institute he founded in Paris (which I used to test the aerodynamics of my Hardelot theatre, the first naturally-ventilated complex building in France, which we shall shortly visit).

The wink in the hybrid name reminds people - within the bounds of judicial nicety - of the brand's origins and heritage: it is supposedly a contraction of Eiffel, SAE and Fougerolle, but instead sounds much more like a gerund, a verbal-noun form of the genius builder's name. The suffix -*age* in French means the same as -*ing* in English, meaning Eiffage is actually Eiffing, personally-branded action. *Eff-ing hell*, Gustave might have thought…

So why would a perhaps dodgily-monikered con-glomerate claiming the biggest and most innova-tive steel and concrete projects in history feel the need to disfigure my sleepy village? The answer lies uphill on the ridge leading to the Mont Saint Romain, where a gash now disrupts the tree line on the horizon. Like many construction majors, Eiffage has felt the need to keep up with the times and increase its interests in wood construc-tion. The metropolitan corporation had sent out its lorries (heaven knows how they read the tiny script on the road….) to the hinterland to ex-tract and stock up on 'farmed' Douglas-fir which had been planted in serried ranks (as an invest-ment) about forty years previously. Clear-cutting a swathe through the village's domanial forest (managed by the Office National des Forêts), they punctured the continuity of our woods and left behind a waste of uprooted stumps - as if they had been Orcs from The Lord of the Rings bent on eco-destruction. During a dawn walk on the ridge with a local farmer, he pointed out that they had not paid attention to the wind-break effect of this stand of trees, and several had been needlessly blown down behind. It chills me every time I walk through this battlefield that a faraway hand could descend and scrape our land-scape with not so much as a care. It makes me think - in my bones and the pit of my stomach - of the far vaster devastation wrought on Amazonia on a daily basis, displacing whole peoples like the Runa we encountered previously.

As a Paris-based architect with an (increasingly large) foot in the country. I stand astride both ends of the chain of supply and production. On one foot I order wood for buildings, commonly Alpine Spruce for cross-laminated timber structural panels; on the other I see the effects of primary extraction. Burgundy oak and beech - also harvested from around our village - sadly often ends up exported to China to make floorboards, and is then reimported to Europe at a hefty markup, having belched out vast amounts of maritime diesel fumes on each leg of its trip. My spread-legged stance gives me some insight into the effects of my choices as a designer; woods regrow, but every time I specify a solid panel, somewhere there will be a bald patch for some time. I have to trust in the goodwill and intelligence of the foresters I source from, lest I be the cause of another country-dweller's anguish in Bavaria or Finland.

French President Charles de Gaulle famously exclaimed 'how can you expect me to govern a country which produces 286 cheeses?' One might therefore reasonably expect that France's forests are equally diverse and resistant to order: indeed, they are 70% privately-owned, a mongrel mix of gnarled broadleaf and relatively young upstart firs, arrayed against market-crushing phalanxes of standardised Teutonic and Nordic spruce and pine. Even the Canadians can smell blood: a friend - who exploits 2,000 contiguous square kilometres of boreal pines in Quebec for engineered timber products - can import and undercut the French market and expect his suckered épinettes to grow back quickly without replanting. As a frequent participant in industry bodies across Europe, I discern a difference between radiantly confident, prosperous Austrians

Cited in 'Les Mots du Général,' Fayard (1962)

154

and Germans and the slightly anxious French, unsure about how to make industrial and economic sense of their mongrel woods.

Marion Waller - head, from 2015 to 2023, of architectural innovation at Paris Town Hall, and an expert on ecological questions - has stated that any city has first and foremost to acknowledge its debt to the hinterland. The all-wood structure of the Olympic Village she is planning north of Paris will obviously not have grown on site, it will be cut far outside the city gates. Metropolitan decisions affect the country intimately, and we should try to be sensitive to them (the same obviously goes for food). To help orient this process we will look at a much closer circuit - which has been whirring for a few decades now in western Austria - as an example of how we can harmoniously, consciously and joyously coexist with the forest whilst living from it. In the process we will see that we can learn from the trees we use; they can help us become better humans, creating closer civic and social structures, as well as self-sustainingly beautiful architecture which brings us into enduring contact with the matter of the natural world. And this will be a family affair.

But I would like to start with a story of personal growth towards empathic exploitation of the forest, towards making my own clearings as a mature person, no longer overshadowed by my father's protective branches.

A Puppet
(Bavarian Spruce)

There was an extended period of limbo following my father's death in which his belongings were hastily shuffled into the garage, allowing the house to be viewed by potential buyers as a 'lived-in' but depersonalised environment. 'Declutter' was the watchword of the estate agent, no small task with a hoarder like him. In a frantic weekend of unseasonal February warmth his CDs, paintings, books, clothes, kitchen items and plant paraphernalia were frantically boxed up and stored, mostly for subsequent transit.

The garage already had a story to tell, having become the depository of several layers of narrative. There was a smear of my own semi-unwanted detritus, objects leaving a trail backwards in time through adolescence to my infant teddy bear (a gift from my maternal grandfather the day I was born), objects not significant enough to have accompanied me on various intercontinental migrations, but not so meaningless as to have been cast aside. There were bits and bobs of my father's relegated belongings, and the distilled, final elements of my mother's life, her dearest photographs and belongings, including my brother's school tie and photographs of me at various stages of my life: etiolated, spotty and diffident in school uniform, long-haired and idealistic with my future wife, beardy and filled-out now. There was an LP of Verdi's *Te Deum* in which she sang in the choir, and a heap of photos and documents recounting anterior generations, people in large flat hats staring into a camera for one of the few photo ops in their lives, the unknown looking out across time towards me, with oddly familiar features. Apart from questions of space, some of these objects were in the garage because they were too highly charged for my father to be able to share the house with them; he missed my mother so much that he only displayed a photo of her in the final weeks of his own life, twelve years after her death.

In one of the boxes I came across a wooden toy. Touching it for the first time in four decades opened the floor of time beneath my feet and transported me down to my nine-year-old self encountering it for the first time, on a late-spring holiday in Bavaria during our last year in Germany. It was a detailed, gaudy skeleton marionette, all its bones carved from pine wood and hollowed through to allow a set of strings to articulate movement and even - with a flick of the handle - a frightening decomposition of its members. The head could be swivelled, the jaw made to speak, the legs and arms to jig. Dem bones, dem bones. There were also my brother's two dragons - a mother and baby - who had thrillingly flappable felt wings and articulated jaws with protruding canine (or dragonine) teeth.

These were the only childhood toys to wash up on this beach of memory. I think I exhausted the possibilities of the skeleton fairly quickly; he (I will call him 'he' through personal projection and identification) required an audience, a narrative, perhaps even a theatre, in which to come to life, and it was rare that I could muster any of these. The sketelon's agency was depleted by an insufficiently rich context, but he got to stick around because he was made of a noble material, and was intrinsically interesting as an ingenious articulated object. He was the result of individual, crafted care, rather than mass-production, and somehow this maintained him as part of a set of objects held together by subconscious and chance factors rather than conscious curatorship.

The buckets of Lego which held far more fascination for me as a child had not made it this far. It is hardly surprising - given my eventual profession - that I should have favoured them, but I was not interested - as many children are - in making towers or castles, sentimental play-houses or vast, colourful piles. I was obsessed with refining possibilities and performance, ostensibly the mindset of an engineer, but it was actually the ethical elegance of form, of distilling most from least, that I found deeply satisfying, as I still do now, in the richness and tumult of the design process. This predilection resulted then in a minimalist, sleek car which destroyed any and everything my poor brother could range against it in our smash-up contests.

French philosopher Roland Barthes' short (but deeply resonant) chapter on toys in *Mythologies* laments two things: the propensity of toys to impose a miniaturised adult world on children, and their loss of quality as they were increasingly made from petrochemical products. He says:

> They [toys] are all reduced copies of human objects, as if in the eyes of the public the child was, all told, nothing but a smaller man, a homunculus to whom must be supplied objects of his own size...The fact that French toys literally prefigure the world of adult functions obviously cannot but prepare the child to accept them all, by constituting for him, even before he can think about it, the alibi of a Nature which has at all times created soldiers, postmen and Vespas. Toys here reveal the list of all the things the adult does not find unusual; war, bureaucracy, ugliness, Martians, etc. It is not so much, in fact, the

imitation which is the sign of an abdication, as its literalness: French toys are like a Jivaro head, in which one recognises, shrunken to the size of an apple, the wrinkles and hair of an adult. Barthes (1970) p. 53

Barthes goes on to reminisce about the disappearing wooden toy compared to omnipresent 'gross and hygienic' plastic. Wood is

> ...an ideal material because of its firmness and its softness, and the natural warmth of its touch. Wood removes, from all the forms which it supports, the wounding quality of angles which are too sharp, the chemical coldness of metal. When the child handles and knocks it, it neither vibrates nor grates, it has a sound at once muffled and sharp. It is a familiar and poetic substance, which does not sever the child from close contact with the tree, the table, the floor. Wood does not wound or break down; it wears out, it can last a long time, live with the child, alter little by little the relations between object and hand. If it dies, it is in dwindling, not in swelling out like those mechanical toys which disappear behind the hernia of a broken spring. Ibid. p. 54

I was very fortunate to have parents who never sought to make me into a microcosm or a model; I was never a mini-doctor, builder, pilot or anything else, except in my own fantasies. Open-ended toys like my Lego (and -a favourite- wet sand, in which I moulded Zaha Hadid-esque caverns) allowed me to figure my journey out for myself. You might think, though, that the skeleton's poetic woodiness might prolong his life following our re-acquaintance. Alas, he didn't make the Barthesian cut, he was doubly mortal.

One of the saddest rituals following a modern death is that of taking carloads of stuff to the tip, having made often very emotional casting decisions beforehand. Disposing of the body is not the end: there is far more material waste to manage (as ethically as possible) at the end of a contemporary western life. In every municipal tip I have visited across Europe the same story plays out: skips full of sorted waste, a huge landfill skip for the non-specific or intractably hybrid, and an Ali Baba's cavern of intact objects (many of them discarded toys, almost exclusively in plastic), usually a chaotic and overflowing place, a multicoloured morass of things in some hope of resurrection by adoption; not quite thrown away, but in limbo or purgatory. Divorced from their adopters after the brief spell between intense desirability and programmed obsolescence, leaving a trail of fumes from shipping container transport and hydrocarbon extraction for their fabrication, this plastic Pinocchio workshop aggregates - at a global scale - into a consumerist eco-apocalypse.

My skeleton joined this purgatory, something of a wooden misfit.

There was, of course, a winning team in this deathly casting process, largely composed of my father's most precious objects which are of direct use: books, CDs, paintings, gardening materials and tools, kitchen stuff and some clothes; not to mention the bonsai described at the beginning of this book. In Burgundy we built an armature - like that of an Egyptian pharaoh - to keep these objects alive and buzzing past the divide of death, rather than forgotten in cardboard boxes (as they largely had been in my father's garage): a specific library and listening and reading area, space in a vast storage room with four-metre high wooden doors, and a display wall for his best paintings.

160

The skeleton - whilst judged insufficiently mean-ingful for my grown-up self - had, however, already left his mark, had done his job. As I thrilled with him on our first encounter in Bavaria, I was simul-taneously - and unknowingly - laying the path for a lifelong professional fascination with wood - for all the positive reasons Barthes describes. And - around me then - the Bavarian forest was already starting to grow the infant Spruces which I would harvest forty years later and turn into a wooden theatre near Calais, the kind of place which poor skeleton needed, but never had in his own lifetime.

The Tree-Man in the Theatre (Bavarian Spruce)

The wooden skeleton's resuscitation (and redemption) as an unconscious influence in my life culminated in a single, naïve, fateful phone call to an industrial wood producer in Bavaria: *could they* -against the example of all previous possibilities- *help me make a theatre entirely out of bent, massive structural wood panels?*

Making any building - a bicycle hut, a royal palace, an airport, a hospital, a tomb, a home - is always an act of both destruction and creation. Following the tales told earlier by Vitruvius, Laugier and others, and in the Bible, we know that shelter implies sacrifice, domination, even sin. For Vitruvius, trees were comparable to slaves, not to be cut (or sold) when pregnant. In both cases ('pregnancy' for trees meaning their growth period in the spring) fecundity meant softness and a redirection of resource towards producing future forms, rather than existing strongly in the present with optimal use for enslavers. Construction is preceded by violence: having extracted resource, we must also scrape away topsoil, dig out worms, divert or defy groundwater, and percussively, ritually drive piles to overcome the uncertainties of shifty terrain.

The Ten Books on Architecture, II.9.1

And we depend on trees. It doesn't matter if we're even building in wood. Melting metal requires fire, which may no longer be driven by the charcoal on a forge; but it is still - whether in a canister or in a barrel - fuelled by decomposed, fossilised trees.

Any concrete building necessitates the preliminary construction of a ghost building in wood, a sort of reverse-Rachel Whiteread mould which will vanish once the sludge has set inside, sloughed off like snake skin. Or scraped down and varnished for another round. Or enslaved in a prefabrication production line, indifferent to where the chunky infants birthed from the wooden forms will settle.

My architectural studies (after a degree in English at Cambridge) were - with hindsight - astonishingly unmaterial. There was a brilliant introductory course by the late Lindsay Falck covering - at a gallop - all construction techniques from balloon frame to brick to concrete to tensile, with a few site visits, but that was it. It was as though you asked a trainee chef to work without deep knowledge of ingredients, without reading the labels to see which ones are toxic, full of additives, high in sugar, highly processed, from unreasonably far away, grown in festering water. Chefs assemble food on a plate and then it goes down the hole; as architects, our meals endure, age, patinate and weather, and require upkeep, transformation and maintenance. So we need to learn far more: a temporal dimension, endurance, reheating, rehashing, repair. We also need to know more about how things are produced, transformed, transported and assembled, because this may generate the greatest environmental impact (positive or negative) of our work. Buildings are routinely designed today to consume very little energy, using technology (efficient building systems, renewable energy sources, heat pumps) and passivity (orientation, airtightness, thick insulation, solar gain and protection) in equal measure. There is clearly not much point, however, in keeping the heat off for longer if the building's bones have meant the burning of many tonnes of lime (for concrete) at 900 degrees Celsius. Imagine your minimalist mountain villa: concrete exquisitely poured, perfectly insulated, triple-glazed, ultra-efficient wood stove. Now think of it as - instead - a vast cauldron of crude oil burning for days on end, spewing black smoke over the valley. Because that's what it is. It won't be your valley full of the smoke, however. You will have 'externalised' the problem, in ecological parlance….

In my studies there was an emphasis on social, philosophical, urban and historical questions -all very important for making informed choices as a citizen-space maker. Materials were evoked for their cultural associations, strength and shape, but not their footprint (this was the early 1990s, an innocent bygone age by comparison to ours today). However, concrete silently got the upper hand, most notably through the omnipresence of Swiss architect Le Corbusier, as well as local Philadelphia lad Louis Kahn (who had been chair of the school twenty years before). I was taught by Guillaume Jullian della Fuente, Le Corbusier's last studio leader, a great and protean painter and architect in his own right. Corbusier's language employed freely-formed plans, long window openings, chunky pillars, monolithic exteriors and flat roofs: all the preserve of concrete, the material that can go anywhere, be anything. Corbusier did not entirely suppress the qualities of wood, using rough planks whose grain would be immortalised after their self-sacrificial moulding. It is worth noting that he was a pioneer of concrete building in the tough postwar years, and the workforce making the moulds was sometimes unskilled, the means of support (rickety wooden scaffolds) rather basic.

The Timber Handmaiden

The term 'Brutalism' used to describe his (and others') work is derived from the French 'béton brute' or raw, exposed concrete. He vaunted material honesty and primitivism for ethical reasons, especially later in his career, when he was obsessed with bones, rocks, and the shapes and flows of internal organs. He forgot to salute, though, the ghost bride, the wooden handmaiden who gestated his buildings in her empty moulds. And I failed to notice her too, seduced - as a young, hesitant designer - by the ease of drawing the contour of a concrete wall/façade/ floor/roof/pillar without having to concern myself with how it would be made on a building site, by humans using various tools and collateral materials.

I moved to France after graduation partly to extend this infatuation with plastic, minimal forms. The mid-90s saw a short-lived hegemony of Le Corbusier mini-ayatollahs, preaching his 'five points of architecture' (I've stated them above, more or less) as if they were the Gospel, or demi-Ten Commandments. There was a distinct professional downside to this orthodoxy, however: architects could remain dumb about construction (as I was), enthralled only with historicism and formalism, churning out building plans quickly with barely any details, then handing them over to the grown-ups (engineers and builders) who would tutor them to full size. There was also a mirroring industrial organisation, the big building groups all holding substantial interests in concrete sourcing, production and transport. It was a co-dependent addiction to a nasty product, big industry keeping architects on a short leash, everything going to plan so long as we didn't try anything too fancy or out of the ordinary. Even today - in supposedly more enlightened times - I still occasionally encounter a concrete acolyte stuck in the 90s, endlessly incanting - like the Ancient Mariner - its virtues of simplicity (for him and his company), fire resistance (not as good as you might think), cost (again, good for him) and longevity (not so good either, requiring regular cleaning).

You won't hear anything about inflexibility, bad hygrometry, building site noise, dust, pollution, excessive transportation, beach destruction, externalised costs, and so on.

The widespread, democratic (and sometimes dumb) tradition of timber stick construction in the United States had led - for me - to a hands-on familiarity with wood. I could make simple furni-

Board-marked concrete column in La Tourette refectory

ture, some fairly complex architectural models, and basic shelter for myself, learning more or less by osmosis. It had not occurred to me to try the same in concrete, or metal: wood is a deeply permissive material, the bar for entrance very low indeed (*just get cutting…*). Once basically competent with bits of pine, the subsequent possibilities for ascension to the rarefied realms of France's quasi-mystical *Compagnons du Devoir* are almost limitless in terms of tree species, skills and knowledge. After a brief spell working for Jean Nouvel - whose buildings are brilliant, sublime, shifty (and rarely inviting to the touch) - I was in limbo, somewhat primed to respond to the boyhood wooden skeleton tapping on my skull, waking me up to his own world of possibility which had remained dormant to my professional faculties.

There was another stage in this initiation, which would - slyly and unexpectedly - introduce a mood, an ethos, a set of preoccupations which have proved to be searingly relevant as the world has heated up and convulsed in pandemic. It would involve lots of bamboo.

Chameleon Background

When, twenty years ago, I first met theatre director Peter Brook - who was one of the most brilliant creative and spiritual minds of our time - he spoke only in practicalities, theory-free and devoid of portent, obfuscation and pretension. Walking through the streets of Paris, he would note that a certain pizzeria was losing business at lunchtime since it had been thrown into shade by a large horse chestnut tree coming into leaf: he was allergic to the abstruse and abstract, and committed to the real, the real as a vehicle of the invisible. This was a function of his craft: on stage, things have to work immediately, and a live audience gives immediate, transparent and democratic feedback. You ignore this at your peril, and deciding not to ignore it leads you into a kind of alchemy of objective, physical effects. Like a chef balancing salt, sour, sweet and savoury, Brook would balance loudness, rhythm, distance, direction, colour, texture, timbre, brightness, and even smell. I found him to be extraordinarily sensitive to space, able to apprehend instantly the myriad factors in a room which might conspire to making his job as a communicator and storyteller easier to perform. His judgements were straightforward, but based on a very deep intuition. 'Some spaces are conducive to communion,' he said to me, 'and it is the architect's job to figure out what makes them so. One thing is sure: it can't be neutral. Man without a background doesn't exist.'

Interview with the author, 1996

The many performance spaces which he chose, transformed or created from scratch over the years all have the sense of being an active background, a sensitive participant, a supportive presence. Chief among them, the Bouffes du Nord theatre in Paris (which he found whilst it was in the process of being demolished in 1974), has a peculiarly elastic quality. Damaged by fire and water, neglected by its custodians, its wounds unbandaged, it had (and has) a quality of being partly natural and partly artificial, with no clarity or boundary between the two. Brook exploited these qualities for nearly fifty years, tuning this chameleon space - without transforming it, relying purely on the audience's imagination - into a forest, a palace, an Indian garden, a Russian cherry orchard. It is universal, but its universalism is rooted in its specificity, and its specificity is shifting, dynamic, ambiguous.

The presence of an actress or an actor on this stage does not rely on their exceptional qualities alone, as it would in front of black curtains: they are supported, part of a bigger system from which they draw strength. In other words, it is an *ecosystem* (literally, *a housing -or home- system...*) in which the human exists because it is in relation to other forces, a living background. And not because - like Leonardo's Vitruvian man - it hogs the space, frowning, spread-eagled, falsely autonomous, alone on stage. If Brook's theatre is a world in miniature, it is not a bounded world: the magnificent walls of the Bouffes du Nord - red, scarred, crumbling, timely and timeless - are somehow also transparent, allowing to filter inwards an outer world of great complexity and protean kinship. It is in keeping with this particular mood that the bodies present on the stage are, themselves, not homogeneous. Without an attitude of tokenism or equal opportunity, Brook assembled a troupe of exceptional beings from England, France, Japan and Africa, all of whom have said that they identify with this space through the prism of their individual heritage and traditions.

Bouffes du Nord
Theatre, Paris,
2010

When Brook had to introduce 'settings' into this space, they never took the form of curtains, flats or realistic rooms and exteriors. The only things that this extraordinary chameleon will accept are suggested locations: a carpet to denote a room in a house or a doctor's surgery, or - more powerfully - a floor of earth to transport us to the mythical India of *The Mahabharata*. 'Natural' materials seem very much at home in this ecosystem: the latter show had water, fire and many accessories and props made of wood and bamboo and vegetal textiles. These objects were conferred a sense of reality by the Bouffes, manifesting their own inherent force and dignity -like the bodies of the performers. This force would be sapped away on an elevated stage against black flats; the audience would have a greater effort to undertake to thrill and to empathise with them.

In *A Magic Flute*, a distilled version of Mozart's magical opera, the only added element to the stage was a series of bamboo poles held upright by being anchored on simple metal plates. Very rapid to move around, they could be organised in a grid to denote an ordered, urban space, grouped symmetrically to form a palace façade, or arranged haphazardly to represent the forest through which the lovers must pass as part of their trials. Bamboo not being a common material in eighteenth-century Vienna, it nonetheless did not jar or seem foreign. It is - a bit like the Bouffes - a matter of artifice, a pragmatic substance still used for scaffolding in Hong Kong, a living-dead being shorn of its leaves which can invoke human and non-human character. It is then and now, immemorial and contemporary. It was used - as long poles - in rehearsal exercises by the company, creating linear geometries, communal radius, slow, coordinated rituals requiring exceptional concentration and empathy. Some actors would use it themselves in their own workshops, transmitting its chameleon power to other groups. On one occasion, customs officials pulled aside an itinerant Brook performer and asked what on earth he was doing with twenty bamboo poles for luggage. With a disarming wisdom he replied: 'it's teaching equipment.'

Ghost Tree-Man

The actor in question, Sotigui Kouyaté -a stick-thin, towering, willowy Burkinabé originally from Mali- was one of the most extraordinary beings who haunted the Bouffes' stage. He told me that he felt perfectly at home there as it had something of the character of an African village square. Unschooled in the artistry of western 'performance,' Sotigui would *manifest* on the stage rather than *act*. As the ghost of Hamlet's father he was utterly, palpably, naturally dead, ghosts being a matter of everyday life where he came from. He could also do an uproariously funny church lady or - though he never touched a drop - a poignant, stumbling drunk. He also incarnated spiritual figures such as Prospero and the Senegalese *Tierno Bokar* - a role that was written for him by Brook and Marie-Hélène Estienne; and he was devastatingly convincing as the man-god Bhishma in *The Mahabharata*, slowly en-

Brook's company carrying out group exercises with bamboo in Africa, 1974 (screen capture from company rehearsal video)

171

acting his death under his own control, relinquishing the life force as a bee flying overhead let a drop of honey fall on his tongue. When Sotigui himself died (in 2010), Brook admitted that he felt no sorrow for him: he had lived - like Bhishma - an exceptional life attuned to others, and was still strangely present. Brook said to me at the time:

> I first saw him in a photograph that Marie-Hélène Estienne showed me: he was standing next to a tree, and he had an extraordinarily tree-like character himself, both physically and personally. He was inseparable from his own African soil, rooted in its social, cultural, family and spiritual structures and traditions. He was deeply animist in the sense that he saw and sensed, as a matter of course, the continuity between the visible and invisible worlds, between inner spirit and external tradition. At the same time, when he was in the context of the west, he was totally open to the world around him, seeing it clearly in all its good and bad qualities, but without ever judging or becoming hostile. Like a tree, he was unbending in his core, but reaching out, responsive, quivering in reaction to every fine current with which he came into contact.

Telephone conversation, May 1st 2010, quoted in The Guardian, 'Sotigui Kouyaté Obituary,' May 2nd 2010

Sotigui himself said (in a 2001 interview with Cynthis Guttman):

> I come from a culture where nature is very important in a person's life. Your soul is first incarnated in a tree, then in an animal and then in a living human being. Some people are even named after trees. All this means everything in the world is alive. Unfortunately, humans increasingly think they're the only living beings on earth.

In French, you can point to someone and say "there's a person." In several African languages, when you say "person," the word is followed by something that means roughly "the person of the person." That is, each human being comprises many identities, which are in fact other people. Daily life is about discovering all these beings within. This can only happen through meeting other people.

A few years after Sotigui died, my father phoned me, excitedly wishing to describe a very memorable dream. Following a serious stroke in 2012 he had some significant handicaps of perception and language: he could only write with great difficulty and had to use a stick as his right side was seriously weakened. Already rather circumlocutious, conversations post-stroke tended to resemble cubist charades; he would even (early on) speak in Latin and German, languages he had not used for decades. Very oddly, I was deeply helped in this process by having seen (dozens of times) Brook's production *The Man Who..*, based on Oliver Sacks' eponymous book about patients suffering from brain lesions and strokes. They were not presented as case studies:' names of disorders were never used, but their unique brain architecture revealed - in the total mosaic of the piece - the miracle of 'everyday' perception. My father's language aphasia was one 'disorder' represented in the piece, helping me to riff along with his burrowing attempts to bring to the surface fragments of meaning, and stitch them together. We developed a game of scat singing whilst driving (distraction was useful), trading four bar breaks of sometimes nonsense, sometimes meaningful syllables. Our game was adopted by his doctors as a healing technique.

My dad explained to me that he had written out a significant word from his dream and wanted to share it with me. In the dream he was standing on a beach and a very tall African man had welcomed him near a circular berm in the sand. He explained that if he waited until the next day, a group from around the world would gather there, as it was a theatre. They would be from many countries, but he would be able to understand them all. The man asked him to remember a word, which he had - on awakening - transcribed in vast, scrawling letters, as 'HATAMBHARA.' My father said that the dream had given him great reassurance and a feeling of belonging in the world.

Shortly afterwards I took him to meet David Williams and Sue Palmer, old friends of mine who lived nearby in Somerset. David has written several studies of Peter Brook's work, and was close to the company in the 1980s. When he handed over one volume - with Sotigui on the cover, performing as Prospero in The Tempest - my father burst into tears, exclaiming 'that's the man from my dream.' We were deeply moved, but hardly surprised, having already encountered for ourselves the transparent facilities of the tree-like man in question.

There is no reasonable, rational explanation for this dream. Most importantly for me, it gave comfort to my father as he faced his own death; he felt part of a bigger community, a polyglot community recalling Babel and the multiple tongues of Pentecost.

Time Bending

All of which leads us back - rather circuitously - to the naïve phone call I placed to a Bavarian wood industrialist in 2013.

My firm had been selected to participate in an architectural competition to design France's first neo-Shakespearean theatre, close to the wide sandy beaches of the Cote d'Opale south of Calais. The competition brief imposed untreated wooden cladding on the outside - a requirement of the historic monuments authorities, as the building would be situated in a listed site adjacent to a ruined Norman castle. The prescription meant that the building's outer skin would age, weather and patinate quickly, and attain a commonality with the bleached-grey stones of the castle. Having felt the tapping of the wooden skeleton's finger some time earlier (we had started to design buildings in wood with very high ecological ambitions), I felt the urge to go beyond the historic requirements in this case.

I had studied the Elizabethan theatre in depth, visiting the archaeological remains of the Rose as they were unearthed in London in 1989. I sensed something magical about the wooden bones of these buildings: they were simple and vernacular - pragmatic, feet on the ground - and also with their heads in the ether, replete with cosmic symbols, incarnating physically a world axis with a substage full of subterfuge and slippery ghosts, a mid section where normally constituted people moved around, and a lofty balcony where kings or spirits could draw us upwards. In other words, rather like a tree.

Another aspect had fascinated me: one of the first Shakespearean theatres (called The Theatre, in Shoreditch) was dismantled following a land rights dispute and carried across the river Thames to be erected on Bankside, where the Rose and Globe would later grow. Even more excitingly, a proto-Shakespearean theatre (a banquet theatre, with three galleries and a canvas skin) had been carried from London to near Calais by Henry VIII's court, and erected for a week's revelry with François 1 at the Camp of the Cloth of Gold. This was only a few kilometres from the site of the proposed theatre. So this solid, timber theatre which was both democratic and numinous, was also a sort of high-tech product of expert carpentry, a robust demountable prefab.

Facing the one-time opportunity of making the first such building in France, we started thinking about what the craftsmen of Shakespeare's time would have done with the wood technology of today. Cross-laminated timber was invented in the early 1990s, and was well on the way to being able to replace concrete as a primary planar construction material. It is a form of engineered timber made by gluing successive layers of solid wood strips perpendicular to each other. Unlike plywood - which is made of sheets unrolled in a single, long, unfurling cut from the trunk of a tree - CLT maintains the thickness, grain, knots, resin and presence of the wood. Because it is two-directional it can be used indiscriminately as a floor slab, a roof, a wall. Large

Hardelot Theatre CLT panels being assembled on site, April 2015

176

holes for windows and doors can be cut without affecting its structural capacities. As dumb as cardboard, it promised to wreak vengeance for all the sacrificial wood buildings ever made for pouring concrete, by occupying the same space the concrete would have filled up. There would be no need for preliminaries.

A quarter of the weight of poured concrete, it also promised great advances in building site procedures: it could be delivered in very large pieces (stacked together on a lorry, as big as the trailer would allow), all openings pre-cut, electrical conduits chased in, bolted or screwed connections preformed, and lifted into place by a truck-based crane, without the need for monopolising a slow-moving tower crane. The developments were eye-watering: a high-rise building's structure could be erected at the speed of a floor per day, with ingenious drop-in click-joints for columns. The prefabrication would be computer-controlled to tiny tolerances, and the material would be tested and certified for measured consumption by fire. It would effectively protect itself, designed with a sacrificial char layer which would prevent the collapse of the building (or delaying it by a regulated amount of time).

The one weakness arose from what was otherwise a benefit: its lightness meant that there was often insufficient acoustic mass to prevent the transmission of impact noise through floors and walls. It tended therefore to be clad in layers of other materials, or topped in concrete or clay for floor structures. Consequently, its manufacturers (who would all end up producing an essentially standardised product) didn't care too much for appearances, allowing basic and intermediary grades to feature regular knots from the spruce trees most commonly used.

The walls of the Bouffes du Nord have a similar capacity to the wooden walls of Shakespeare's Globe to project us from here to there in our imaginations. You can call them an environment, a presence, a reminder that were are not merely existing in a human-centric, controlled environment. Processes of growth and decay are continuing all around us, and creators like Peter Brook have seized on this as an essential, dynamic ingredient in any space which corresponds to our natures and to the world. There is no human without a background. There is no human without an environment, an oikos, a home. A forest. A forest clearing.

It was immediately clear to me that the walls of our future Shakespearean theatre had to be both alive and contemporary, precise and open, in this manner. They should manifest character, accident, time, indoors, outdoors, past, present and future. They should be the flesh of the building.

Hardly anybody bothered to build with exposed CLT, and not just because of the knots. Everything would have to be detailed more carefully, and assembled with great precision. Something destined not to be present would have to be treated differently. The building was also round. The plans under development showed varying radii with curved plates sailing past each other in concentric sequences, generating an exciting range of in-between spaces. I was convinced that medium-grade CLT with all its flaws was exactly the kind of material we needed, and that it should be the only material, as singular and exposed as late period Le Corbusier concrete. I picked up the phone and called the major producers (all in German-speaking countries). Only Heinz Thurik of Züblin timber (then a division of Metsawood) did not say no immediately. After a short hesitation he said 'of course, we can make this work. But it will take some thinking.' We completed our plans - and the core identity of the whole project - taking this on trust.

A couple of years later I found myself in Heinz's factory near Augsburg, where a series of what looked like small hump-backed bridges were present in the yard. These were the positive moulds for the theatre's wall structure, elements that might in the past have served for a concrete building instead. CLT is made in the Metsawood / Züblin factory in a partly-automated process. Strips of solid wood, either 27 or 17 millimetres thick, are dumped from a large basket onto a large rubber sheet on a flat bed of about 6 by 20 metres. A skilled worker kicks them out into one plane, and then does a kind of shuffle with his feet to pack them together. He jumps off the neat sheet he has just shuffled out, and a robot arm descends and squirts glue evenly over the surface. The same procedure is repeated, but at a 90 degree angle (the *cross* in CLT; I will - for once in this book - avoid the obvious appeal of Biblical metaphors here). When this wooden lasa-

Top: the positive forms used to set the curved panels

Bottom: Hand-finishing the theatre's CLT panels

179

gna has been settled in 3, 5, 7 or even 9 layers, the rubber sheet reveals its purpose: it is a high-strength vacuum bag which is sealed around the wood and then emptied to minus three times normal atmospheric pressure. After a couple of days' curing the bag is opened and the lasagna has set into a solid slab, glue oozing out over the edges. It is then placed on a rolling production line, adjusted to be perpendicular, and cut into a crisply-defined panel by a computer-driven saw. It is also possible at this stage (for flat sheets) for the same robot saw to cut out windows and doors and rout out channels for structural attachments and electrical conduits. In many cases it can then be shrink-wrapped and simply loaded onto a lorry with a bar-coded identification of where it will fit in to a building-sized 3 dimensional puzzle. Perhaps a day later it would be dozens of metres in the air, supporting other members of its panel-community, ready to shelter human activity.

In the case of the theatre the process was less automated: the solid spruce strips had to be laid by hand and bent to the forms of the hump-back bridges (the smallest of which had an eight-metre radius, about as tight as could be realised; this formed the inner wall of the auditorium). Once in place the whole element - mould included - was put in the vacuum bag. Cutting it to finished dimensions was also trickier than with a flat panel: these giant smiles would bounce and flatten slightly when lying on their backs. They had to be placed on the cutting bed by hand and eye, the slightest deviance from the curve resulting in a useless, trapezoidal panel. Astonishingly, these bouncy forms would recover their precise, intended shape when lowered into place on site. Sanded - by hand - perfectly smooth, they had a new-born perfection when they first arrived in their resting-place. After a few hours only in the summer sun, they would start to tan:

leave a piece of tape on the wood from the packaging, and it would transform into a bikini line when removed later. White and pure, the Bavarian wood was alive, (or at least) subject to biological processes of dynamic transformation, coloration, hygrometric variance and the weeping of resin (the latter still continuing years after construction was finished).

Talk to an Austrian builder (as we will in the next chapter), and they will be at pains to explain their methodology for caring for wooden panels whilst under construction. This often involves building a protective structure around the new-born panels or an umbrella over the building site. At the very least it involves large tarpaulin sheets and a careful eye on the weather forecast. Wood reveals cultural differences: there are different ways of doing things with the same living matter, different ethical and financial imperatives. Many Austrian, German and Japanese colleagues who have built in France have complained that wood is not sufficiently respected here. For Japanese in particular (as we will see later) it is a treasure of almost sacred value; they are anguished to see it abused.

In the case of the theatre building there was a disconnect between contractual stipulation (to protect the panels at all times) and real life as it played out on site (against my express wishes and orders). There was a three-week summer break in which the theatre was left exposed to the elements (coastal rain, very regular). It was grey and stained when construction restarted, meaning that we had to take the perverse decision to renovate an unfinished building, sanding - as best as possible- the oxidised and stained layers of wood. The result was not homogeneous; it would not have passed muster back in the wood's homeland. I was rather distressed: this could have been avoided, and sanding a whole building whilst trying to finish it with other trades was a bruising experience. One could only, however, go with the flow: the wound had occurred, one had to figure out how to live with it. I don't recall thinking about the degraded walls of the Bouffes du Nord, but it slowly dawned on me that something positive had occurred within the greater negative: the building had been forced to open itself to time and to the outside. It would never be entirely a container, there would always be a sense of it having been invaded, or open. In their imperfection, the walls had an unplanned dynamism, an ambiguous character which might actually be useful.

There was an inside-out character to the general conception of the building. Unlike Shakespeare's urban buildings, packed into Renaissance London like circular spaceships landed gingerly in the only available terrain between rows of houses, the Hardelot Theatre had the choice of location within a large and verdant site, itself adjoining a large nature reserve. We started our design work from the inside, imagining the relationship between a performer and audience, and worked back from the outside, dreaming of the kind of structure which could serve to negotiate this encounter between silent, enclosed intimacy and windswept greensward embraced by a curving allée of horse chestnut trees, with a stand of old beeches in the centre of a lawn. The diagram that resulted was a bit like a peeling onion, with the central cylinder of the auditorium dissimulated by leaves which shifted asymmetrically. The building did not declare its internal axis to the outside, it was sculpted to house the functional bare minimum of entrance and servant spaces. This allowed some interesting encounters between CLT panels: a narrow, 9 metre-high, top-lit curving staircase with raw wood on both sides; slipping spaces allowing perception out of the building into in-between zones almost all around; and a small foyer with a glass roof which generated the sense of penetrating deeper into a forest glade. The auditorium itself had controllable natural light from a clerestory which extended two thirds of the way around the drum. We had to give a codename for the completion (whose final phase was anonymous). We chose 'Clearing' ('Clairière' in French).

There was only one problem. The existing natural site with its majestic, gnarled trees covered in ivy, its distant views towards the Channel coast, its swampy lawn, was more than a little intimidating. No matter how sensitive we had tried to be to the surroundings, carrying wood through from outside to in, tightening the volumes to a visual minimum, we just couldn't situate it comfortably. It was too big, too chunky. My collaborator Solveig Rottier came up with a ruse: we would surround the whole thing in a diaphanous cage of bamboo poles, generating a pure cylindrical form around the accidental volumes in solid wood. In this way it would look like a sort of oversized Peter Brook exercise, vertical and radiating poles indicating a communal centre. She made a computer model with the bamboo on a separate layer of data. We turned it on and off:

bamboo here
bamboo gone
bamboo here
bamboo gone

It helped. A bit. We couldn't decide, but we had options. Having perceived the site for several weeks on a (comparatively) tiny computer screen (with abundant photos, videos and plans), it was obvious that the real thing needed to be experienced one last time (and very late in the day before the competition hand-in). I rented a car and drove the three hours from Paris with my small Shiba Inu dog Suki for company. Arrived on site, I loaded myself up with a sheaf of plans and images and started pac-

ing around. No good. Suki then broke for a rough patch of nettles and brambles at the base of the stand of trees we would have to cut down. I beckoned her. She was headstrong. She stared at me. I got impatient. Same hard stare. She was beckoning *me*, in fact. I went to fetch her, and -standing next to where she sat- I turned around. Instant revelation. She had chosen the most subtle and strategically important place in the entire site, something which would never manifest on a plan or a photo. At the base of a gentle downwards slope, she was in a protected spot, but a spot from which she could survey the entire site, from the gatehouse, far away to the horizon, a foreground of two curving trunks perfectly framing a third, more distant one before the ground fell away towards a lake and the forest towards the sea. Ridiculously Japanese. And, to the right, the castle itself was barely perceptible in the periphery of vision. I patted her on the head, noted the spot on my plan and took a photo. Two years later this became the view outwards - back into the landscape - from the front door of the theatre. Unencumbered with my brain-clouding thicket of dimensions, diagrams, distances and reductive photographs, this deeply sensitive creature had given me a powerful lesson in the limits of self-perceived exceptionalism. I was behaving like Viollet-le-Duc's arrogant time-travellers Epergos and Doxi, mocking the attempts of the first dwellers with their privileged hindsight. She, however, was much closer to the condition of Vitruvius' proto-humans, curious, instinctive, open to the example of all forms of life, not perceiving themselves as suddenly 'created' or shamefully 'fallen' into mindfulness. I felt - and still feel - deeply grateful to her for this lesson. Our building was situated, its character locked in place, and very clearly needing the veil of skinny poles to render its presence subtle and ambiguous. I phoned Solveig and exclaimed 'bamboo here!' Suki was applauded at an inaugural event and cited in the fusty, mainstream architectural press as co-author. The theatre was named best wooden building in the world.

Midway between canine revelation and Bavarian spruce-shuffle at the Züblin factory, I was given the opportunity to present the building to another dog-lover (and I rather regret not taking Suki along). I have described the encounter in my book *Common Sense*, but one crucial detail escaped me at that time. Queen Elizabeth II wanted to see - on the occasion of what she had said would be her final state visit to France - the doings of her subjects in the hexagonal country. The Ambassador, the canny and brilliant Lord Peter Ricketts, had proposed the future Elizabethan Theatre of the Château d'Hardelot as having a nice consonance with the visiting monarch. I presented the building in the form of a large wooden model made by Solveig and Nadia Raïs, complete with a removable roof so she could see the seating and balconies inside. She asked some rather unexpected questions: what kind of wood for the columns? What's the diameter? The façade wood? How is it treated? CLT? What's that? She knew her stuff, and she wanted the deets.

See the chapter 'The Uncommon People'

It took a while for the penny to drop, partly because she was always coy about her agency, her reach. She was - in fact - the apex forester, past or present custodian of vast swathes of Scottish Sitka Spruce, Maori primal hardwood, Australian tropical bush, and - not so long ago, through the Firm - chunks of the Ulster Plantation, as well as vast areas south of the border. She was conspicuously missing from the Latourian inverted earth-diagram, owning the sea bed around much of the British Isles. She was the Critical Zone Queen, from bedrock to canopy. The whole conversation was cast in a new light: suddenly I felt like a potential customer more than a subject: one wink to the Lady-in-Waiting

Photo (facing page top): Claire Morris

Photo (facing page bottom and four following pages): Martin Argyroglo

and the samples would be fetched from the boot of the Roller outside. I was impressed.

Her forests and clearings predate her and have outlasted her, and are curated by many hands and minds. She was the dynastic apex of a polyform (and sometimes dysfunctional) forest-family, giving a particular character to swathes of the landscape, its vegetal life, its non-human dwellers, and the subjects who might subsist from it, or suffer the runoff of monospecies-planted, acidified soils in their streams and lakes. If you are a stag roaming her moors, you did well not to get into her crosshairs.

The forest is a family affair. Unless it is one of the tiny patches of old-growth, primal woodland that remain, it is inevitably a four-dimensional tapestry of its owner's (and exploiter's) intelligence -or lack thereof. You have to have your shit together to live well with the forest, and for the forest to live well with you. In my own singular example here I am aware that a blank spot was left on a Bavarian hillside (for a few years at least), the kind of blank spot which depresses me in my home valley. The Spruce - which is not well-exploited in France, and only suited to certain parts of our climate and landscape - had to travel a long way. On the other hand, by committing this wood to being enshrined in a building we had fixed about 20 tonnes of greenhouse gases into its veins, knots and fibres: unless the building burns or rots, releasing the CO_2, it will remain there, a genuine benefit when we consider that embodied energy is the biggest factor at play in most buildings' impact these days (remember the concrete villa earlier?). It's significant but small. What would happen if the landscape was peopled by a clan who really knew what they were doing, both during the life and the transformation of the wood to our uses? We have to go to Austria to find out.

A Family-Forest
(White Pine, Larch
and Ash)

At the top of an Austrian Alpine valley, architect Herman Kaufmann leans against an exquisite wooden time machine. Above his head, framed by fine, grizzled pine shingles, is the window of the farmhouse room in which he was born in 1955. Stacked back behind that room is a sequence of chambers which trace his family's industrial history to the present day. These chambers grew larger and larger as their fortunes prospered, like the spiralling alveoli made by a nautilus as it grows according to the Golden Ratio. The sequence culminates in the vast, brand-new Montagehalle which produces up to six prefabricated timber buildings a year, birthed in perfectly finished apartment-sized chunks which will be trucked away and stacked on site into their finished form, requiring only plumbing and electrical networks to be fixed together.

Stretching behind Hermann's head, this apparatus collapses the time between traditional hand-craft and digital innovation, between ancestors sawing planks and today's world-leading capacities for

Hermann Kaufmann outside the room in which he was born

fast and precise prefabrication. To his right is the modest house where one family custodian per generation has lived on site to oversee affairs; it now has its fourth occupant. This is abutted by one of Kaufmann's first designs, a 1980s workshop which is skylit and enclosed for warmth and silence. It is abuzz with an army of ant-like carpenters, each knowing perfectly his own task, and coordinating silently with the others to lift and shift the bones of a future apartment building. This hall is flanked by the small, breezy, original studio of his grandfather, giving onto the exponentially greater volume of the latest hall, which enables world-class innovation in wood design and fabrication.

Indifferent to this spatial and industrial crescendo, the adjacent village of Reuthe keeps a low profile: two-storey wooden houses meet the fertile plain without fuss or ceremony, fenceless gardens are loosely-defined and seep into the agricultural fields. Around this scene, beyond the cultivated ground, clinging to a shadowy mountain, legions of trees look down, witnessing the fate of their kin as they metamorphose into human shelter inside the hangars.

The village is one of 22 existing in a loose constellation in the rollercoaster valleys of the Bregenzerwald above the cities of Bregenz and Dornbirn. A beacon of craft culture for decades, also dotted with family-run, world leading technology and equipment brands, the Bregenzerwald (and the greater Vorarlberg region to which it belongs) has the typical shape of many Alpine zones: small, autonomous villages with slightly varying culture, each occupying the farmland radius from which it can reasonably live; flat, fertile valley bottoms framed by pasture slopes, which are the preserve of mid-season cows; and higher slopes which are nibbled only in the summer. On steeper and higher slopes the

Kaufmann Company
Montagehalle, Reuthe,
Austria, Johannes
Kaufmann (architect),
Konrad Merz (engineer)

beasts cannot occupy, the landscape is entirely forested until the scree and ice of the mountain makes lush life impossible.

Something in the air is different here, though, propelling the Vorarlberg into becoming a global mecca for lovers of wood craft and construction; it is a similar draw for those curious about a balanced co-existence with a territory, especially in gastronomy. Down on the shore of Lake Constance, the utterly improbable summer opera festival wows audiences of 7,000 people a night with massive dancing structures rising from the water. (It all started with the war-traumatised Vienna Symphony Orchestra deciding to retreat here and play on barges facing the shore). The festival, a source of local pride and beneficiary of the region's prosperity, is presided by a local lad (Hans Peter Metzler) who prides himself as being one of the inventors of Bluetooth.

Hermann Kaufmann, his family, and their exponential facilities, are protagonists of the wood-craft revolution of the Vorarlberg. Son and grandson of carpenters (Hermann and Ernst respectively), Kaufmann was building things in wood from childhood, helping his father shore up and transform barns, lending a hand in the sawmill, getting to know the local varieties of trees (predominantly white fir, spruce and ash). Hermann Kaufmann senior married Anna Kaufmann (no relation), making them Kaufmann squared, double-barrelled. The pre-Kaufmann-Kaufmann Kaufmanns had lived modestly from wood craft, taking what they needed from the surrounding forest. Passing this on, overlapping between generations, Hermann the younger became - following his uncle Leopold, 22 years his senior - the first architects of the family, meaning that they had created a feedback loop in which construction materials could be procured within the family, and the architects making use of them could propose innovations in the fabrication of planks, beams, siding, and also laminated and aggregated elements such as box beams and trusses. Hermann's three brothers also work with wood (his three sisters not; his younger brother Johannes designed the supreme Montagehalle). What Hermann calls the 'close' family is 115 persons, almost all anchored in the Vorarlberg. They're not a family, they are a human forest, communing, making the most of the land's offerings, transforming them into crafted treasures whose influence resonates in a very particular way in contemporary architecture.

Our protagonist's skill is now called upon in Vancouver and Japan, but he has built principally and plethorically around his home region. Driving through certain areas, you pass a kindergarten, a bus stop, a fire station, a hotel of his, every thirty seconds. Down in the plain of Dornbirn he has built an 8-storey wooden office tower to Passivehaus standards; its structure was erected and made air- and watertight in an eye-popping eight days. Further afield in Vandans he has built a 120 metre long, five-storey office slab in a sylvan dell reaching out over a lake, whose rigour, generosity and warmth set the whole valley singing. The building uses local oak, spruce and white fir according to availability and appropriate application; it is a poetic patchwork of territorial capacity. Make the same thing in concrete, and the valley's song would become a scream.

Kaufmann's is a unique situation: most architects would sink into self-emulation or megalomania with such omnipresence. His secret is cooperation and connectedness. His clan-forest have grown alongside him, jostling, sharing, inspiring, holding back from excess. His fellow dwellers have also shaped his work very profoundly. In Krumbach, Arnold Hirschbühl - the sparky mayor of the

Following page:
Top: Meeting room in
Bezau Civil security
Building (Hermann
Kaufmann, architect).

Bottom: Parish
Hall and Library,
Krumbach, Austria
(Herman Kaufmann,
Renée Bechter and
Bernardo Bader,
architects).

1,000-person village - asked Kaufmann to shape - over many years - a subtle civic centre which consists of housing for young and old, a refitted municipal and service building, and a boxy parish hall and library (designed in collaboration with Bernardo Bader and Renée Bechter). The apparent simplicity of the latter is deeply deceptive. You start to understand this by looking down at your feet: the church, situated diagonally across from the entrance up a slight slope, is surrounded by radiating granite paving blocks. Still outside - but under a porch - the floor turns to wood, then back to granite (in rectangular flagstones) in the entrance airlock. Then, in a vast, minimal hall, it becomes roughly planed oak boards, which meet - without the sticking-plaster of a skirting board - walls of white fir boards, joined by tongue and groove to form a flawless surface which - years after construction - still smells of the forest.

Your feet tell you - through subtle changes in friction and reverberation on these floors - that you have come through a modest but significant transition to a sheltered space in which you are welcome, as welcome as you were (in a more serious and directed way) in the church, but here as part of a broader community. Kaufmann has made vast windows and glass doors which allow you to understand your relations to the sacred and profane currents outside. A lofty stair volume leads to a library upstairs, nestled under a single-pitch attic. This stark triangular volume (the consequence of the most traditional roof form imaginable) feels utterly contemporary. The monomateriality (white fir walls and oak floor) is comforting rather than oppressive. At the far end there is another vast window, scaled to be sat in by children hearing stories, seemingly engulfing the snowy slopes and farmhouses outside. The prowess of 3 by 5 metre triple-glazing has a civic function here (as it does

downstairs): it helps you understand where you belong, and opens you up to where you come from, an experience which sits on a fine balance point between framing and immersion: it is both distanced and close, in a way that undifferentiated floor-to ceiling plate glass (the preserve of much archi-guff about openness, fluidity, democracy) never will be. You can imagine yourself being transported by a story in this room, which already, by its constitution, allows you to be both *here* and *there*.

We architects have a strange way of speaking about construction quality in terms of tolerances (by which we mean what we are prepared to tolerate, contractually, lest a work be refused for non-conformity). We speak of structural and material tolerances, which - from international experience - I have found to vary greatly, reflecting broader cultural questions. In France, typical tolerance for site-poured concrete is a centimetre over three metres, although in practice this can often become five, on the assumption that it will be taken up (and redeemed) by cladding and chunky sills. Slapdash workers in a hurry save money for the contractor; inexperienced, unprincipled labourers cost less. The construction industry is structured around this ethos, architects being neither expected - nor paid - to elaborate large quantities of details giving specific quality. Derogating from this system makes you a dissident, and sets you up for fights on site: people have mouths to feed, shareholders to enrich, and asking for quality often means you stand in their way. Things can get ugly.

This situation extends to architectural education in France, which is largely conceptual and not particularly practical. In my own studio, I often find myself starting from scratch with recent graduates, going back to basics, offering continuing ed. Architects have painted themselves into a corner, allowing developers and politicians to unpick our role until it is reduced to the choice of facade elements from a catalogue (with stringent price restrictions attached). We nonetheless find ourselves burdened by the bureaucracies of planning and construction management, often with ineffective levels of authority in either case. I have sometimes found that the only thing I can do to maintain quality on the building site is to shout, sometimes at the top of my lungs; and you tend to save this for when it is really needed.

At the end of our visit Hermann Kaufmann took me to his home, a stolid villa on the outskirts of Bregenz, rather conventional from the outside. The interior, however, was a song of love to the forest and its gifts. Without volumetric extravagance, every corner, every detail was crafted with exquisite care. 'We had to take our time,' he told me, 'because we wanted to get the best people, when they were available.' A semi-circular staircase with dovetailed cantilever anchors leads to the sleeping quarters upstairs. The finishes are varied: a guest room is decked out in ash, with achingly precise joints, even in areas which are not immediately visible. Kaufmann used ash because the specie is disappearing locally through disease. He kept one suffering tree and aged it for use here in this one room. One tree, one room, one guest. Two hosts: one human, one arboreal.

The French three centimetres' 'tolerance' would be - in the Vorarlberg - a gulf of infinite space, the vacuousness of Munch's Scream, the unnameable, the unthinkable, Anish Kapoor-grade emptiness. Their extreme precision (no skirting boards; impossible to insert a fingernail in mitred corner joints) does not speak of intolerance or obsession, but of extreme confidence and civic strength. The absence of expansion joints tells of a profound knowledge of wood, and faith in the suppliers (probably friends or relatives) who have dried it out carefully. The absence of finishes, varnishes, beading, bars, rails or signs indicating desired behaviour, radiates acceptance of and faith in one's fellow-citizens. Britain, by contrast, is becoming a hi-vis country, driven by (understandable) accessibility concerns and (perhaps excessive) risk-averseness. The entire country will end up painted in fluorescent yellow stripes at some point, as if to eliminate all possibility and therefore all risk.

Wood is both strong and fragile: the prevalent pine walls here are soft to the touch, the grain standing slightly proud. A spilled cup of coffee or a careless scuff would ruin an entire wall. The fact that it is so often exposed in all its weakness -and is consistently cared-for, whether in a kindergarten, a fire-station or the parish hall- shows that a subtle but profound covenant has been established and applied. The forest has given of itself for human purposes; it still speaks, though; it is morally alive, and the microcosm of countless porticos and thresholds which do not bear the scars of ignorance or indifference carry a far greater promise: that this living matter will be cared for at a much greater scale. A much-loved doorstep is a talisman of the balanced cohabitation with the green sentinels who will grow all round and provide future materials for us, without being over-exploited. The wood whispers alongside us, making the daily gestures of careful entry and passage into microcosmic, ritual acts of care for the whole world.

Wall joinery (ash wood) in guest bedroom, Hermann Kaufmann house, Bregenez.

Staircase adjacent to Fire Engine Hall, Civil Security Building, Bezau (Hermann Kaufmann, architect).

Ablution of the Field-Gods (Sakaki)

The spirit was *invisible*. As per. So was his girl-friend. But they had their limits. Having impelled rice and soy to emerge from the ground for a whole season, they were invited to luxuriate in a bath, which posed some problems of protocol: entering the water would mean risking a surfeit of ineffability. Blank on blank, invisibility dissolved. Clash of nothingnesses. Transparencies cancelling each other out.

So they manifested conjointly as a pine branch, and took a dip in the warm water, breaking the surface tension, filling the air with a resinous perfume.

Earlier, whilst still out in the fields, they had been lured towards this needly dunking by a phalanx of humans fanning out into the landscape. Each human carried a sakaki leaf in a folded paper pocket, murmuring to incite the divinities to snuggle inside. When one person sensed a pregnant pocket, the hunt was called off and the group reassembled. It then processed to the bath-house of welcome, reverently carrying its sleepy invisible treasure. In the house a feast for two awaited: bounteous fish, beans, rice, turnips, grilled wild boar. It was laid out on a raised platform with the humans gathered around, a leader and two assistants bowing down before the bounty. Once the gods had feasted and begun their winter sleep, it was the turn of the attendants to this transformation to fill their bellies and converse about the year behind and the year ahead, comparing notes on the incursions of wild boar. They milled about on outdoor wooden platforms floating above the rice paddies, or in the timber interior, feeling the embrace of the forest behind. In an in-between world between uncontrolled and cultivated land.

This scene could have taken place in the 13th century in exactly the same material conditions. Instead, it was during the autumn of 2015 in the village of Mii in the Noto peninsula, and the gathered crowd were not monks but professors, jet-set architects, designers, social workers, rice farmers, daycare workers, chestnut farmers, charcoal producers, craftspeople. The domestic hosts were Kiichiro and Yuki Hagino. The former (known as 'Kibo'), is a globe-trotting architect, teacher, and expert on earth construction. His wife Yuki is a product designer, pastry chef and ecological activist. According to Yuki, they were hosting this ritual not out of nostalgia or respect for the past, but as a signal to the future. The ineffable pine-gods were carrying an important message about how better to live in balance with the whole world.

The ritual is specific to the Noto area, a rural peninsula sticking into the Sea of Japan about midway along the Nippon archipelago. Noto has been buffeted recently by depopulation, demographic imbalance and a serious earthquake (in 2007); there is concern about the rural way of life surviving, and perhaps clumsy attempts are being made at a national level to rebrand it for tourists nostalgic for a simpler way of life than the frenetic buzz and long working hours of Tokyo.

The specific capturing, bathing and feasting ritual I have described is not formulaic, but a product of Kibo and Yuki's imaginations, in collaboration with their neighbours. It is called *Ae no koto* - the feast of reception - and occurs twice a year, marking the sleeping and reawakening of deciduous and arable plant life. Yuki and Kibo are (a bit like me) rurally transplanted metropolitans, Tokyoites issued - in Kibo's case - from a great industrialist family. Long-time residents of the United States, they experienced a severe reverse-culture shock on returning to Tokyo. Kibo - eldest son of his family - renounced the inheritance of his father's metallurgical business and went native, deciding to build a wooden house abutting the forest, in an area where they had no prior links. They were blown off course by the earthquake, which caused Kibo to pause his own construction and apply his earth-building knowledge in helping urgently to restore traditional barns damaged by the disaster. Even if they have 'retired' to the country to concentrate on local detail, their personal and psychological hinterland and frame of reference are global. It's hardly surprising that their very local acts resonate far beyond: the particular social life they have created in relation to plants and the land attracts interest and visitors from far away (like myself). Their home is a focus for community gathering and discussion, and an internationally-important centre for studying biodiversity. In the clumsy neologism, they are 'glocal,' near and far, with fine roots and wide horizons. Here and there. A bit like the spirits of the field.

For Kibo and Yuki, questions of human community and non-human biodiversity are indissociable. The jolly anthropod gatherings - at which everyone has a task, chopping wood or vegetables, cooking or cleaning - are also used - in high summer - as the format for minute, collective investigation of the non-human crowd in the surrounding fields and forests. People disperse and return with a *Wunderkammer's* worth of the insects and plants they have bumped into on the way. This treasure is laid out on the terraces and subjected to a census. The resulting tally gives a detailed idea of how the non-human world is getting along, season by season, measured across both the worked and free landscape. Yuki Hagino has said that the totally of life in their confined valley is the *real* divinity they are invoking: the totality of life in a place, bound together by complex relations of interdependency and competition for resources.

2015 field-gods (in front) resting adjacent to a display of plant samples attesting to Mii's biodiversity

There is a word serving to denote what goes on in Mii: *satoyama* means 'the product of collaboration between people and place.' In other words, place is a process, process is a place, and the human and non-human are joint agents of both. Ae no koto - which has Shinto origins (of which we will hear more in due course) - is a domestic or family-based ritual dating back many centuries, which essentially celebrates this concept, extending it to a spiritual dimension. In the shadow of World War Two, UNESCO began to preserve significant places and buildings from future damage, developing the World Heritage Site classification. Later, in 2003, it was decided also to include habits and practices in its protection register, alongside physical things. *Ae no koto* washed up in their net in 2008, based on

209

a recommendation from the Japanese government including 29 other practices such as paper making, dyeing and various dances. This gave rise to a certain surprise, it being a distinctly local matter. One local farmer remarked that this made him feel self-conscious as his personal version of the ceremony included coarse jokes to distract the divinity and to make his family laugh. It felt incongruous to him that this was now somehow part of a globally valued heritage.

The farmer's embarrassment reveals the ambiguity of attempts to expose and conserve process, especially those relating to the outer world of other living things. The urge to protect is never pure: in the case of Japan, the motivation to push for UNESCO status arose from a 1999 agricultural law whose third article called for the formation of an 'appreciable' landscape manifesting cultural transmission. Most farmers (including the ones I know well in Burgundy) give little thought to how their recomposition of the land might register culturally or aesthetically: they are in a race to survive, day by day, year by year, victims of increasingly volatile weather, big-business price fixing and demographic changes. Japan has - rather like the Austria of the Vorarlberg - a 'rational' land structure, flat areas cultivated intensively until they meet slope and forest. (Japan is 70 per cent mountainous). The clearing which has been pushed back as far as usefully possible, to the back side of Kibo and Yuki's house, is - for the government - akin to a stage, a locus of spectacle, of husbandry and organisation which should be - by law - appealing to the eye.

The intention - to manifest qualities of process, to render locations attractive, to lure outsiders in tour buses - may have a certain economic logic, but it may also signal the death of the thing it seeks to preserve, by denaturing it, by fetishising a small part, a fixed, repetitive loop of the processes which engender it. There is a spectacular example in the Noto peninsula, a cascade of tiny rice fields on a cliff above the sea, denoted 'the thousand rice fields of Shiroyone' (there are in fact nearly two thousand, some of them barely a metre wide). The myriad field borders are illuminated at night to the enchantment of tourists, but this is an intervention against their nature, as they would normally be continually in process, rebuilt from year to year, mutating without respect for their appearance. The former Japanese Prime Minister Koizumi Junichiro made a stop at the Shiroyone site as part of his farewell tour, and noted - ominously, I feel - in the visitor's book

> Even if we don't make rice any more, we must preserve this landscape!

Cited in Kikuchi (2015), p. 257

If the heritage landscape is - for a head of government - merely scenery, as shallow and as insubstantial as the wood flats in front of a Western saloon on a Hollywood back lot, it may well behoove us to turn to Yuki Hagino's all-encompassing eco-divinity to restore a sense of substance, to bring depth and life to our relations with the forest and the land.

Forest Communion

Kibo and Yuki's village of Mii is practically all outskirts. There is a soupçon of a high street, with houses on both sides, a few offices (including Kibo's) and a social club for the ageing population, some of whom may spend as much as five decades in retirement. Otherwise, people settle along the liminal zone between arable land and forest, in a wiggly line which goes on for hundreds of thousands of kilometres around the whole Japanese archipelago in exactly this format and relationship.

Mii village, rice fields and adjacent Hinoki Cypress forest

The distinction between the two land uses is a simple matter of topography: the forest starts where the ground first slopes, the rest of the land is kept flat to allow rice and soy cultivation in parcels of land which can be flooded in a controlled manner. There is a clear demarcation between flat and sloping land as - respectively - cultivated, producing food, and untamed, the province of beasts. (This vertical diagram is -generally speaking- reproduced in cities, even conurbations as vast as Tokyo and Kyoto, where humans build out the plain to its mountain fringes, and venture no further.) The main societal problem in country villages like Mii is the wild boar, which refuses to respect this boundary and invades paddies, digging them up, sometimes rather thoroughly.

Satoyama - the term we saw previously used to denote collaboration between people and place- is also a generic term for 'plain.' The forest is a shiftier matter, carrying two nomenclatures, whose

212

qualities can overlap. *Hayashi* denotes a 'working' forest comprised of trees planted for human gain. These are essentially cedar (sugi), cypress (hinoki) and sawtooth oak (kunugi). The other name, *Mori*, denotes the entirely free forest, ostensibly separate from human agency, populated with broadleaved trees and feisty beasts like boar and deer. In practice, *Mori* often contains 'cultivated' trees, sometimes planted generations ago and taking up residence without fear of the chainsaw. Despite a prevailing attachment to myths of primeval purity and continuity, very much of Japan's vast forest area (68% of land use, compared to 13% in Britain) has actually been cleared and replanted at several times in history. Cedar and cypress *Mori* are rather different from the broadleaved forests of origin myths: they are very dark and vertical, disorienting and repetitive monocultures. There is not the welcoming canopy and breathing space of - say - a zelkova forest.

Most recently, the urge to regrow, to generate resource rapidly after the Second World War (which was devastating for Japan), resulted in massed, overcrowded plantations of reliably productive cedar which have, in many cases, not been exploited and allowed to grow freely. A normally managed forest might start this way and then be thinned out after a couple of decades, allowing the wood to produce tight, hard growth rings initially in what would become its heartwood, and then develop to full size.

There may be a character of trauma, of tightening the belt too much, to this serried planting, which I can't help but relate to the regrowth of my local forest in Burgundy after the same war. The principal menfolk - all engaged Résistance fighters - were taken by Nazi troops on one fateful night in January 1945 and later killed, some in the concentration camps. They were arrested in the restaurant next to my house and mustered and taken in sequestered lorries in the garage which has now become my wife's painting studio and my wood workshop. The village population became predominantly female, and the different resulting energy took a less invasive, less intensive approach to working the land, reducing the area of vineyards, allowing forests to recover and regrow into the form I know today.

Forest and mountain being contiguous in Japan, there is a tension between the perception of benign forest gods and more capricious mountain gods, responsible for great storms, sudden flooding and landslides as expressions of their anger. The balance and harmony of the Japanese landscape is held to belong to a tripartite collaboration between the passionate mountains (who capture water), the peaceful trees (who tame it) and the plain-dwelling humans who are able to use it in a steady flow from the hills to predictably husband the land.

Mori and its adjunct *Chinju no Mori* are fundamental places, atmospheres and ideas in Japan. *Chinju no Mori* is a specifically Shinto appellation which refers variously to: a sacred primeval forest, never touched by human hand; a temple precinct as a real-estate whole, comprising forest, buildings and other elements like car parks; and a common term for both primeval and productive landscapes around a temple. It is a shifty term, whose truest meaning resides perhaps in an *idea* of sanctity, a sanctity whose precise boundaries and component parts are unimportant. It's all about a *feeling* of the vegetal world, without linguistic or topographical precision. It's not a matter of scale, either: even in great Metropoles there are microcosms of the foundational forest associated with temples, in the form of small clumps of trees known as *shinboku*.

On Mii's wiggly outskirt there is a specific example of this fluid form and meaning: the local Shinto 'temple,' the Gongen Shrine Ichinosaka, is not a building but a single, venerated zelkova tree. Ceremonies are held at its feet in a small grove; a stone Tori gate denotes a threshold before this arboreal presence, a here and there associated with the tree. The officiating priest is an amateur local, and - unlike a Catholic priest or an Imam - makes no claims to being an intermediary with the upper, invisible world. He is merely an enabler, a reciter, a servant of the community.

If community bonds between insects and humans are held to be important (even sacred) by our contemporary celebrants, there is some foundation for this in Shinto mythology. It's worth turning back to the beginnings to unfurl this question, to the eighth-century foundational texts (the Kojiki and Nihon Shoki). In both texts, the earth was formed of heavier matter condensing from the heavens. The gods used their sky-bound agency to stir up - with a spear - the heavier matter of the earth until it began to find a form. A drop of salt formed into the island of Onogoro. Descending to this first land, the gods Izanami and Izanagi begat the other islands of the archipelago and implanted a sacred pillar (*Ame no nishira*) as their first constructive act. Circling around this column, they became aware of their attraction to each other and of the complementarity of their genitals. They then reproduced polytheistically and made human children (the first of whom are deformed, owing to an insufficient subordination of the female Izanagi to her husband).

So far, so Old Testament: there is a swirling of matter into choate form, and a loss of innocence around a totem-tree, and some dodgy gender politics (although at least there is a numerical balance of the divinities, it's not just the big Guy with the beard pointing at things he transforms). Shinto, however, relies very little on dogma and on scriptural interpretation: there are not legions of scholars debating every word of these texts and using them as the justification for annexing other people's land, or for razing forests. It has grown into a folk religion, in the sense that individual traditions are developed and guarded by the family, the folk; every home is sacred, in its own way, with a freedom to invent and choose, and even to blend with aspects of Buddhism (which is often invoked, for example, for very serious occasions such as funerals).

A further origin myth (vernacular, rather than related in the short founding texts) states that the forest is infused with spirits in an undifferentiated manner. Shinto sacrality is not fetishistic of the centralised, obsessed with unique objects, places and events. There are no toothpick-sized fragments of an ür-cross venerated for their narrative and material singularity, no world-centering Kaaba to be circled around for days at the conclusion of the Hajj. In Shinto mythology, the sacred is evenly suffused throughout the Mori and all its agents and inhabitants (which explains the emergence of individual tree-shrines like the one in Mii). However, human experience of the sacred is said to have emerged socially in natural forest groves or *yashiro*: where the trees had thinned out, people gathered, and spoke, and shared their veneration. There was no need to shape, to cut, to formalise: spiritual energy flows through everything, pantheistically. Everything has its place without cutting, burning, or any other form of transformation.

This account is obviously reminiscent of the one in Vitruvius we examined earlier: in his story, humanity is born into a forest clearing which allows them to face each other and start to talk around a centralising fire. There is a significant difference, though: whilst both Roman and Shinto traditions are somewhat animist, Vitruvius' first humans had to be concentrated into a clearing made by the destruction of fire (albeit naturally or accidentally produced fire). In Japan, the groves are ordinarily occurring de-densifications of the forest, implying space with a centre. It is as if the forest parts slightly to allow humans to find their space, without the need for an event, for agency, or for any intervention, whether divine or human.

Self-nature

Japan's noted contemporary philosopher, Yoïchi Nakamura, puts it thus:

> Japan is the only country in the world where there has been a long connection between forests and civilisation. It is a fact that there are no other such countries in the world; it seems like a miracle.

Cited in Rots (2017), p. 112

Resident for several months in Japan in 2015, I sensed quite strongly this exceptionalism - and simplicity. And I drank it in, and felt jealous. Versed in tortuous western debates (especially of knotty ecological questions being examined by Bruno Latour and his entourage), I saw 'nature' as something almost impossible to describe, bent out of shape by centuries of capitalism, monotheism and philosophy. In the Anthropocene, it's awfully hard for us to say what is not somehow man-made; every single thing is contested, must be debated, weighed, treated with due delicacy for its complexity. Latour cautions against even using the word 'nature' (he throws in 'local' and 'global' for good measure): its meaning can slip to include cosmic bodies, opening too wide, too vague a frame of reference in what is effectively a verbal trench war with the deniers of the climate crisis. Terminology is the first weapon in this war, and if we see ourselves as 'global' inhabitants, space-travellers on a solid sphere, we risk losing sight of the extreme fragility of the inhabitable earth when it is measured vertically: we exist in a tiny varnish on the planet's surface, a few thousand metres from bedrock to unbreathable high-altitude air. We have to focus our aim in this war, be very specific about what we want to defend.

No such problem for my Japanese friends, it would seem: nature is simply our extended community of living neighbours and the places they inhabit and make. The concept is not problematic in general and academic discourse, the natural world is held to be conceptually stable and clear: everyone knows what it means. Etymologically, there is a delicious catch, the word most commonly used (*shizen*) denoting 'spontaneous being' and also - to some degree - the self. In other words, there is no inherent contradiction between 'nature' and 'culture,' 'human' and 'other.'

'Nature' in Japan is continuous and ahistorical (or at least conceived of as such), beneficent (despite regular earthquakes) and full of agency and personhood. You don't mess with it. When I suggested suspending some freshly-harvested bamboo stalks (with leaves intact) upside-down in an art installation designed to express our perverse view of the world (and also to point through the earth from Kyoto to Paris, on an axis of two great climate agreements, and on the very day in 2015 when the Paris agreement was signed), I felt a great reticence from the Japanese collaborators who would need to help me complete this artefact. They were polite and did not oppose my idea, but I sensed that - by effecting a conceptual twist, by upending the order of things - I had deeply troubled them. They took it down as soon as they could after the inaugural event.

Nature is - of course - not at all, in fact, ahistorical in Japan. There is no primeval forest. Shinto has not existed smoothly for centuries since its origins; it has been brought into focus and into play for reasons of political opportunity, especially at the end of the 19th century when it became important to develop a cohesive national identity in the face of the external forces unleashed by opening the country up during the Meiji Period. The forest was used very consciously (and artificially) to generate a national identity linked to specifics of land. The veneration of stable Nippon nature also went hand-in-hand with the brutal exploitation (by Japanese interests) of far-away logging sites in Indonesia, a colonial externalisation of need. Shinto - a native and nativist religion - also has the benefit of lacking Buddhism's Chinese origins: it is only Japanese.

Despite all these provisos, there is a great deal to be admired (and envied) in Japanese attitudes to the forest: they possess the framework for an emotional attachment to the total living world which is not hierarchical, patriarchal or centralised. Every household can experience their own version of this kinship extending out into the dark of the trees; people can invent and transmit their own rituals which serve regularly to remind, relive and renew these connections. There is a gentle anarchy to the situation, and also a modesty which means that the focus can be sustained. This, in turn, is more likely to lead to outer, greater-scaled actions which will allow us to live in scale and harmony with our terrestrial context: it is easier to propose the hardships and constraints on our expansive lifestyle if you can see your nearby tree as a being not that different (or less sacred) than yourself.

I am also not entirely right in stating that Shinto has been parachuted into the modern world for questions of nationalist identity politics. There are many rituals besides Ae no koto which have existed in an unbroken line from very distant times, especially in the far southern islands, and some of these are indeed exceptional and astonishing. I find it interesting that many Japanese - including those whose job it is to research and deliberate such questions - find it comfortable to exist in a positive, agnostic degree of floating enjoyment of a cubistic, non-dogmatic, frequently self-contradictory heritage. The truth is roaming in this intellectual forest somewhere, to be discovered and defined for oneself and one's kin. Once found, it will not be any more or less relevant than anybody else's. This not only saves an awful lot of bother (centuries of religious war, for one); it also allows a diffuse, personally responsible attitude to the near and farther world which -in one way or another, whether we like it or not- is under our stewardship and tutelage at this point in history.

I would like to broaden our scope and look -in brief succession- at a wide range of rituals and places which fill out the picture of this kaleidoscopic attitude.

Opposite: just-completed Shinto temple in the Dai-Jingu Shrine, Kyoto, 2015

(below) the author harvesting bamboo, Kyoto (photo: Kiichiro Hagino)

221

The Murderous Sky-Tree (Hinoki and Douglas-Fir)

Sanmon gate,
Nanzen-Ji Temple
complex, Kyoto

The solid cypress pillars supporting the *sanmon* or entrance gate temple of the Nanzen-Ji complex in Kyoto are so massive, so enduring (originally 13th-century, rebuilt (after a fire) contemporaneous to Shakespeare's 17th-century carpenters), so astonishingly direct in how they meet the earth - their trunk fibres resting without ceremony on a bulging granite pad - that I have come to see them as a kind of macrocosm in their own right. This relationship developed over a months-long series of daily visits, including a certain amount of caressing and hugging of them. I had twigged that they might be ascribed with microcosmic properties, the notion of the axis mundi, the sacred trunk linking heaven and earth, supporting the sky, being common to many cultures. In this case, however, they hardly seemed like a metaphor or stand-in: perhaps they were actually doing the job. One of the originatory Shinto texts, the Koji-ki, contains an aphorism well-known to Japanese architects, which goes

> I stand a thick shrine pillar on a solid rock at the bottom of the ground, and raise Chigi to the gods of heaven.

Chigi is the roof apex, the highest member in a heavy wood frame. This incantation (attributed in the text to the Emperor Jimmu, himself mythologically descended from the sky) is commonly used by Shinto priests attending - as they habitually do - to the groundbreaking of any new building in Japan. You can often see the traces of their work, even on banal suburban plots: a future three-bedroom house would have its outline drawn in ghostly string on the gravelly site, with some ashes of an offering resting in one corner. The pillar is obviously loaded with more than kilonewtons of force: it also bears the relationship with the sky.

The Japanese are famously venerative of old arte-facts (like Nanzen-Ji's pillars): broken ceramic pots are carefully reassembled using glue paste laced with gold dust (the art of Kitsugi), the breakage be-ing emphasised as adding to the aura of the object rather than diminishing it. An even more poignant culture emerged from the poverty following the Second World War: with a paucity of raw materi-als, tiny, exquisite toys were made from aluminum recuperated from crashed warplanes; and kimonos were made of scraps of denim and other cheap fab-rics. It is therefore perhaps surprising that some of the most famous wooden monuments in Japan are ritually demolished and replaced according to strict cycles. The most famous is the Isé shrine, which is surrounded by a very particular kind of *Chinju no Mori*, a working forest of hinoki cypress which - every twenty years - metamorphoses into the main, most sacrosanct temple hall or Naiku. Shinto tem-ples like Isé are often kinds of architectonic clear-ings, fenced off against the forest with inner courts of increasing holiness; in the case of Isé - in a ritual process which serves to denote impermanence or *wabi-sabi* - the forest is partly eaten away by the temple, turning into acultured, planed timbers. It goes without saying that the ritual in question is of great and elaborate beauty, each trunk being carried with veneration into the complex for erection as architecture.

At the Suwa Grand Shrine complex in Nagano Province there are four freestanding raw, flayed tree-trunks named Onbashira. Their origin and signification is fluid and misty like much Japanese theology and mythology: they might relate as far back as prehistoric tree-worship, they might be abstract totem-poles, they might also draw inspira-tion from Confucian ideas of the five elements and their interrelation. One thing remains sure: they are replaced every six or seven years (following the

Chinese calendar), along with - as at Isé - the entire building of the western treasure hall or *Hoden*. So far, so *wabi-sabi*: what distinguishes Suwa, though, is the particular form of the ritual used to gather the new trunks onto the site. Starting high up in the mountains, sixteen firs (or larch or cedar) are selected, cut, stripped of bark and branches, and the ceremoniously dragged to the shrine site in a ritual known as *Yamadashi*. This involves crossing rivers and - most spectacularly - descending steep mountain slopes. In these phases - a kind of earth-ly landing of the trunks, a freefall towards their stone pad prescribed by the Kojiki - the ten ton trunks are given agency and freedom: they slide, as is their wiggly wont, down the mountainside. They land on earth as they see fit. Stranger still, these impetuous celestial javelins are ridden like a rodeo bull by a large crowd of men, many of whom have been killed during the ceremony, crushed to death by the heavenly pillar. There is a rubbernecking popular-culture aspect to this, rather like the run-ning of the bulls in Pamplona: the risky, Lilliputian tumbles are broadcast on television (and were in-corporated in the opening ceremony of the 1998

Nagano Winter Olympics). However, the danger is real, is accepted and is nonetheless repeated. Japan - persistent hunter of whales - is perhaps the only country to have developed a blood sport in which humans are regularly killed by plants. Albeit prehistoric, sacred totem-trees falling from sky to earth.

Charles Freger,
Namahage, Oga,
Akita, Japon
From the series
YOKAINOSHIMA .
2013-2015

Cavorting frond-gods

Other Japanese tree-rituals surviving and thriving today bear a protean energy, even violence, which runs counter to the view of the Nippon as reserved, respectful, cautious folk. In the case of the *Raiho-shin* - a largely domestic ritual which takes different forms across the length of the whole archipelago - it is humans who become vegetal, dressing up in palm fronds in subtropical Okinawa, in the central regions festooned in fluffy bundles of rice straw and large, grotesque masks. Dedicated amateurs play the parts of deities who manifest at crucial points of the year: in the chillier north their visitations occur at new year's, the husky gods passing unannounced at private houses, principally in order to scare children into being polite and studious (video documentations show they really mean business, parents happily holding their wailing, terrified children as they are admonished by the vegetal deities).

In the Noto, where we began in a theistic bathtub, there is a particular version of the ritual called *Noto no Amamehagi*, featuring rather refined and varied masks -as might be expected in one of the bastions of Japanese lacquerware production.

In the warmer south the rituals tend to take place around harvest time, and in public space. The *Akusekijima no Bose* ritual (on the eponymous Pacific island) involves creatures with palm frond bodies and high, African-appearing masks who disrupt an annual memorial service, careering through the crowd, smearing red mud onto the passers-by. In Miyakojima, Okinawa, the Paantou ritual involves vegetal deities smeared in dark brown mud running haphazardly through streets, again smearing people (and also walls and objects) with the mud in which they are covered, to ward off bad luck.

These protean rituals are stewarded by citizen-committees keen to preserve the associated heritage and traditions. It is perhaps to be regretted that some bits have been edited out and toned down, in particular the orgiastic, sake-fuelled all-night dancing sessions which were intended to put participants into a state of trance. A trance in which - perhaps - they could actually feel themselves to be vegetal emanations of the forest spirits. Nature as self. God flowing everywhere.

Cosmic fuzz

I was quite surprised - seeing how traditional these forms are - to discover a most contemporary and urban manifestation of this protean nature energy. In the chichi Tokyo neighbourhood of Minami-Aoyama, populated with elegant clothing boutiques and dozens of salons for coiffing your own hair (and your dog's), I came upon something - a small building - which stood out starkly. It was fuzzy, frondy, chaotic, like the Bose deities, a thicket of crazy hinoki poles, all seemingly jumbled together. I quipped to Kibo that I was surprised it could stay so shaggy when surrounded by so many hairdressers. The building in question has a very humble purpose: selling delicious packaged slices of organic pineapple cakes made by the SunnyHills brand. Its appearance - and its ambition - are far from humble. Designed by architect Kengo Kuma, it is a technically daring piece of wooden sculpture, all of the square poles intersecting in perfectly-realised lapped joints, in myriad configurations. It is of interest for our story as a kind of urban clearing, a manifestation - in the most minimalist, uptight, concrete Tokyo neighbourhood - of wild natural conditions, in which one is unsure what is structure, what is enclosure, what is manifestation of purpose. All of the conventional codes of modern architectural legibility are subverted: once

inside, one is unsure if one is actually not somehow also outside; you have to speak to a human to know what to do in there, there are unfamiliar codes of behaviour and placement. In this, it bears some similarity with Zen temple architecture, the garden-space flowing in and out of building and mind simultaneously, the approach designed to disorient and erase the mundane. Here, however, I felt that I had encountered a virtuoso display of something entirely new, and - perhaps - entirely resurrected. For one thing - despite 1700 years of unbroken tradition - it is very rare to see wood used in contemporary Japanese architecture; SunnyHills was reaching back past a rupture as it reached forwards through virtuoso technique. For another, the building seemed to speak of a very contemporary condition of fragmentation, of units repeated ad infinitum (but not in a numbing, banalising way), of belonging to a planetary context which is perhaps careering out of control. The little cake shop (the cake is very good, by the way) was actually a

mighty microcosm, and a charming, scintillating, fascinating, perfectly-scaled and perfectly-executed pair of fingers held up in a gesture of defiance to mainstream Japanese contemporary architectural culture.

Its author is not quite what you would expect from this single building. Kuma is - like his totally different Nezu Museum just down the street - impeccably elegant, laconic, understated, curious and apparently self-effacing. He had a Jesuit education, which is important. He likes Oscar Wilde. He very rarely - if ever - uses the familiar, do-gooding rhetoric of the eco-responsible architect, which is all about problem-solving, demonstrable performance and progress. He has, however, developed a subtle and original discourse concerning this question of 'progress' and how it relates to nature. In his book *Natural Architecture / Small Architecture* he argues that architectural history is far from the forward-marching, technology-enabled smooth ascent that mainstream accounts would have us believe. It is, rather, a succession of irrational spasms spawned by nature's occasional outbursts at our expense, whether the earthquakes of Lisbon (1755) or Tokyo (1923) or the great fires of London (1666) or Chicago (1871). In each case - he argues - society responded by trying to get architecturally bigger, more apparently strong and enduring, in an obvious exercise of denial. The case of Tokyo he takes personally, crediting it with sweeping aside the city's wooden heritage in a regulatory paranoia, resulting in the steroidal city we know today. He told me:

> I was born in a small wooden house, a very flexible building which we expanded over time, we changed the partitions very easily. I still remember the smell of the house, obviously very different from a concrete apart-

ment. I studied at an elementary school of wood as well, something which hardly exists any more. I really want to go back to Tokyo as it was before the second world war, a city with a low silhouette, an amazing street activity. This is the basis of Japanese culture. The Japanese mentality is based on this kind of intimate city: culture, space and material are very much related. Now that we have the cityscape you see through my office window, this totally changes the mentality and the way of thinking. It's not good for Japan: our sensitivities, our delicacy are killed by concrete. This is my motivation.

Cited in Todd (2018)

The litany of past disasters is certainly nothing compared to those yet to come as nature bites us back for having brought her down; we might eventually assimilate nature's future assaults on our coastal cities and agriculture to another paradigm of paranoia, the 'war' on terror, which - following Kuma's reasoning - might cause us to rear up like a wounded Godzilla and throw vast resources at a 'problem' which is unlikely to be thus solved.

What should we do, then? Kuma - admirably, especially for an architectural Champions League player - advocates that we get smaller and do more with our hands; and he leads by example. He writes - regarding the Tohuku earthquake of 2011 and the attendant Fukushima disaster:

> The world is beginning to scale down from big to small. We humans are starting to wean ourselves off big systems (like nuclear power), we're transforming ourselves, actively using our hands and animal wiles to create our nest and energy.

Kuma (2015), p. 28

Kuma credits the stagflation episode of 1990s Japan with liberating him personally in this sense. Having emerged as the author of the overbearingly postmodern M2 building, he was cut down to size and forced to continue through a series of modest regional projects throughout the downturn. These brought him into contact with local craft and vernacular traditions - something he had already explored in west Africa with his teacher Hiroshi Hara - and gave him skill in using locally available and produced materials, especially adobe, hinoki cypress, thatch, bamboo and washi hand-made paper. It should be noted that these materials can have an outlaw quality, existing in a slightly anarchic grey economy beyond the confines of catalogues, markets and standards. Kuma - perhaps uniquely for an architect working at his level - energetically engages government figures to advance regulations and develop acceptance of new materials such as cross-laminated timber.

He literally had to roll up his sleeves and work experimentally in order for buildings such as the astonishingly modest (87.88 square metres!) Takayanagi Community Center to see the light of day - a light which is now lustrously filtered through its painstakingly crafted paper facade. The same goes for bamboo, which he has used as entire culms in the Great (Bamboo) Wall House outside Beijing, employing ancestral (and industrially 'imprecise') oil treatments. A self-described 'guadua gaga,' he even imported containers of the massive Columbian bamboo just to mess around with, to see what could be done. Kuma's marvellous use of adobe bricks in the Toyoura-cho Buddha Statue Repository had a great deal to do with the skill of craftsman Akira Kuzumi, himself a different kind of repository - of millennial knowledge relating to earth construction.

This could appear as a kind of nativist, conservative return to 'roots,' but Kuma actually goes far beyond this, conceptually and materially. He advocates a 'particulate' approach to architecture, meaning that one starts - like the painter Georges Seurat - with the smallest indivisible quantity of an element, and through build-up, repetition and variation, one forms a whole which can never be detached from this smallest module. This is not the British 'high-tech' veneration of the perfectly-conceived, optimised, polished component reproduced ad infinitum to make 'architecture,' but - rather - a way of generating empathy with our surroundings, extending them as an extrapolation of things we can touch, manipulate and make for ourselves (like the flexible partitions of his childhood home). It's a question of that mysteriously unfashionable term, *scale*, and also of our implication within the world as an actor of its substance - rather than as a passive extra in a frozen Euclidian stage set.

It is also - curiously - strongly derived from Kuma's fascination with the thought of Bruno Latour. Latour's former student, French sociologist Sophie Houdart, spent a year examining Kuma's work environment, and describes it as a kind of anthill without hierarchy, full of 'little people' (Kuma included), patiently nibbling away at various problems. Latour has lent Kuma a key concept in his work, that of actor network theory, situating the citizen in an interconnected environment of things and people, all having varying degrees of agency. Kuma remarks wryly that his anthill-office practices ANT.

Latour's thinking evolved substantially since this 1990s idea, specifically towards the question of Gaia, the whole planet working in concert as a vastly complex system whose predictive modeling is becoming rapidly obsolete; the unexpected will become the new norm, within our lifetimes. He has also become increasingly concerned with how politics can address the climate crisis, how we exist as free electrons, as particles, as participants, in a process in which our forms of collective representation are failing to address our greatest existential threat, a threat which we ourselves embody and enact. Latour is proposing to bring democracy down to earth, to reduce us each to a face-to-face relationship with our own prejudices, failings, contradictions and misgivings; to rebuild society one element at a time. In so doing, he argues, we have to renew a detailed perception of the world around us, our individual footprint - our personal clearing - how it is made, how it is not consistent, how it might close in on one side and bulge away on another (perhaps with our kerosene consumption). We are each, individually, as responsible as one another for this crisis, and - with the collapse of existing political models, fragmenting into racist nationalisms, forest-devouring carbofascism, filling its guts with the products of other people's disasters, vomiting poison into rivers and lakes which have supported wonderful societies for millennia - we have to start from the ground up. As trees. In relation and cooperation and kinship.

Kuma's tiny, crazed, microcosmic, beautiful cake shop strikes me as the ideal, counter-intuitive, *natural* non-monument to this kind of necessary thinking. A human clearing. A place of connection.

An Ending: Hornbeam

Previous page: wintry hornbeam and oak forest, Blanot, Burgundy

On the morning of January 8th, 2019, I awoke in a state of febrile tension: something needed to be done, it could not wait. And I had not the slightest idea what to do about it - which is often the best starting point.

My father had died 18 days previously, and he was not yet buried. In England (where he lived) everything stops for Christmas, including death: certificates take longer to process, gravediggers down tools, crematoria put out their fires. He was to be interred with my mother in the Tytherington Memorial Woodlands (a new venture at her time of passing in 2006, now a densely-inhabited pseudo-glade of stringy trees). Mortality is popular these days, and one has to linger (for a month!) for a slot to complete the material journey to a final rest. Death waits for everyman, during the holidays...

On the morning in question things had started to fall into place, both psychologically and bureaucratically. I had awoken - like most mornings then - in a state of panic, my unconscious mind unable to process his permanent absence. This time there had been another note, a kind of half-waking meditation (not really a dream) in which I was aware (*really* aware, not just intellectually) of having been only two cells at my origin. I was merely growth, extrapolation, repetition, a fertilised seed, part of something far bigger than myself. This insight was an important marker on the steep journey towards the upper plateau of grief, where one eventually feels able to move forward with the memory and

traces of the absent loved one. It was also a realisation of an ecology of the self, of every living
thing's extreme simplicity, unique importance and
common, universal character. This revelation was
- in many ways - the seed of this book. More pro-
saically, a funeral date (in late January) had been
confirmed, the crematorium was getting ready to
fire up, there were countless things to be organised.

As an occasional writer of obituaries for The
Guardian (so far, of people I had known personally) I'm familiar with the curious rhythm of passing:
at the moment of life stopping, things go into a
weirdly jerky rhythm, some things bureaucratically
dormant, others screaming for immediate attention, a bit like birth in reverse. I have had - as a
writer - all manner of experiences, including being
drawn into bitter family conflicts in which I had
to represent the objective, historical interests of the
deceased, no longer available for comment; and
also strange lapses, such as notable figures whose
death was revealed to me some time after the fact.
This was the case of the great architect Sverre Fehn,
who had slipped away largely unnoticed, and made
it into print a few months later after some staunch
lobbying (things get crowded - and very political
- on the shrinking obituary pages). In the case of
the Malian actor Sotigui Kouyaté (who - earlier in
this story - visited my father in a dream), a lightning bolt had scorched the telephone network in
the Himalayan valley I was walking up at the time
of his passing. I learned of his demise ten days late,
crossing a ridge and picking up a stray cellphone
signal which delivered a series of distraught text
messages in one burp.

My father's death was not news of interest to anyone
outside of his intimate circle. Nonetheless, a public
ritual adequate to his life needed to be organised
and executed. Christmas entropy had decided that

he would have to be cremated (my brother and I also favoured this idea). The question was, how would he be buried? On that January morning I was at home in our village nestled in a gentle dell surrounded by the Burgundy forest. My father had been there only 7 months before, laboriously painting individual trees in a series of beautiful, wonky watercolours. After a serious stroke in 2012 he had lost much of the fluidity of his perception, and of his ability as a painter (which was considerable). In the beginning of his affliction he used his penmanship to communicate with the outside world, drawing the phantasmagoric intrusions on his field of vision and communicating his wishes and concerns with spindly hieroglyphs. He also drew the desolate scene (a pulled curtain, an empty wheelchair) following the death of his neighbour opposite on the ward.

Towards the end of his life, his previously virtuoso compositional and drafting skills became hampered by a permanently modified perception of depth and colour: where he used to be able to render complex shapes with a few flicks of the pen, now he needed days to assemble (unevenly) the pyramidal roof on our neighbours' house in Burgundy. He had always painted trees with gusto and fascination; in our house, on what would - unbeknownst to us - be his last visit, he rendered them with his reduced acuity almost as a pointillist would, making them distinct, luminous, strong-willed, standing out vibrantly against the village's built scenery. Like Piero della Francesca's holy trees hogging the limelight with Adam, Christ and John the Baptist. Or like the equal-status floating beings in Uccello's Night Hunt, or Shinto deities on clouds, set against a background continuum.

Soil, land, dust, hummus, place, roots, minerals, mulch, compost: these are soft and shifty sub-

stance-symbols for where we like to stand, how we are who we are, where and how we belong and subsist. The same earth-matter can also be refined to a paste, bound in a medium and smeared or soaked onto a flat surface as a way of reflecting back on the same. This is precisely what my father did with almost all his spare time, and much of my own energy after the funeral went into sifting, preserving - and getting to know - these stained pages which he created by the hundreds, noting every aspect of the outer world as it appeared to him, and manifesting a great deal about his own inner world in the process. He was not concerned with ordering his work, with making it known; it was an end in itself, often forgotten once completed. It was to be found in stacks behind sofas, haphazardly hung, in countless folios. It had become a kind of soil, a soft presence which enveloped him, looming off bookshelves, insulating walls, a nest or cocoon.

I have had to turn over this soil - quite literally -, to fork and sift it, examine it, record it and leave it out to air so that others can now engage with it. The only other option was to confine it to the earth, to

Detail of watercolour painting of Blanot, Burgundy, Peter Todd, 2018 landfill, or to the tomb of a cupboard: it demanded a dynamic return. It is not neutral material, it is very much alive, especially to me. It became a happy burden: as I look into these sheets, I can feel his own presence looking back through the scenes he decided to capture. A friend - son of a very famous painter - feels the same: his dad is not quite 'gone,' and the objects left behind develop a life of their own. It's not just a question of degree, talent or worth: there's something quite magical about anybody's will to leave traces, starting with Lascaux.

My dad's own roots are crucial for this: he was not an urbanite, his scale and frame of reference were the small town and its hinterland (a wonderful, magical hinterland in the case of the West Country - from which he came, and to which he returned for ever, after Germany and Lancashire). Unburdened by any conceptual or art-historical education, and unbehoven to any skill bestowed by a professor, his traces are at once utterly conventional and - looking closely, as I have now done - also protean, radical, organic, risky, loving, unstable, elegiac, worshipful.

It's deeply nutritious for me that many colleagues are thinking about the same earthy matters in an urgent way, expropriating difficult terms (like 'soil') from the reductive far right, refocusing thoughts about greater problems of subsistence around the here-and-now, the beneath-the-feet, as we saw in The Upside-Down Forest chapter of this book. This is equal parts ecological, political and personal: our 'footprints' are not just sooty smudges messing up the place: the self-mapping exercises proposed by Bruno Latour show (to me, anyway) that - traced out, taking into account the near, the far, the individual and the common - I am like a phantasmagorical hybrid creature with lengthy tendrils, part static, part flying, part plant, part sea creature, part bird, and - of course - part soil, generating and sustaining other lives, directly or indirectly. You can see my father dreaming of similar hybrid creatures here, part tree, part bird, part rock. He never explained any of this. He didn't need to.

So part of my own process of return, of necessary metamorphosis, of shedding skin, is to offer this up to your eyes, to make any sense of it for yourselves. My eyes are not enough.

The necessary decision that January morning came suddenly, and I could not call it 'having an idea:' it arrived fully-formed from somewhere else: we would bury him inside a tree trunk from the village forest. The woods around us are productive, pollarded hornbeam on the western ridge, cut back for firewood and fence posts for the local vineyards. To the east there are bigger broadleaved specimens and the mature, commercial Douglas-Fir we have already encountered.

Our communal pile of freshly cut oak and hornbeam logs sits on the edge of the village, and is up for grabs for locals. Of course you have to then wait a couple of years before the wood can burn; but in this case I was interested in something that was still oozing sap, full of life, perhaps felled at the same time as my father. S., the village custodian, looked at me with a mixture of pity and concern; I explained the situation, and we had a brief exchange (straight out of *Hamlet*) about the various virtues of oak and other woods for a burial. Having rummaged vigorously through the damp, chilly, mossy mound of nondescript logs, a large, distinct specimen fell on my toe and declared itself for the purpose. The base of a hornbeam 21 years old, it had a muscular, dynamic profile, swelling into squared buttresses like a limb in movement drawn by Michelangelo. I humped it into the back of the car (hurting my foot again), had it cut down in half by the local carpenter, and then took it to be hollowed out by another craftsman further afield, who thought he could do it by chomping it out with his computer-controlled robot arm. He couldn't, and spent two days doing it with a chisel, whilst he was very busy with other matters.

I carried the hollow log to Bristol, entailing an unusual conversation at the airport x-ray. My brother and I filled and sealed it and left it for one last night in my father's house, surrounded by his belongings. It stood up on the table, seeming somewhat alive, and reclined like a baby as we cradled it on the walk to the grave the next day. Straining apart, splitting, full of a life-force, of unfinished business, it was covered in soil for ever.

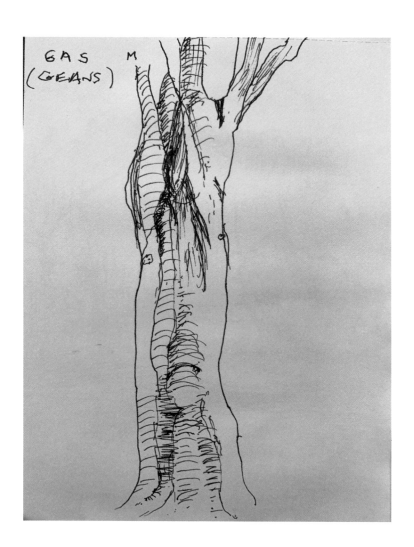

GAS M
(GEANS)

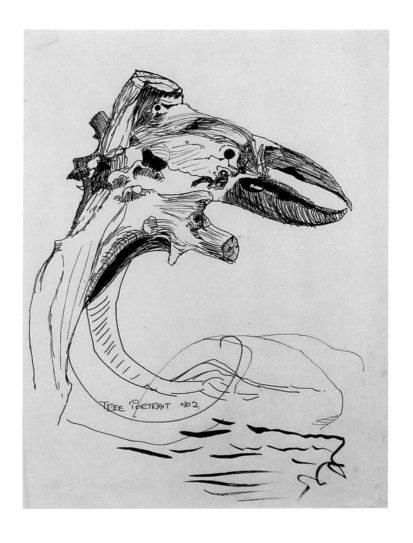

TREE PORTRAIT No 2.

4 preceeding pages:
drawings and water-
colour by Peter Todd,
various periods 1970-
2018

Coda: Interself

I thought that this book was finished. Sadly, I was wrong.

The chronology of writing ended immersed in the Ituri forest, my studio filled with the heavenly, pealing songs of the Mbuti. The process of writing had permitted me to inhabit forest worlds vastly different to my own as I overcame the intimacy and intensity of my forest-father's death. I had been able to see how close we in fact can be to the Mbuti, perhaps not in actual manner of living, but in awareness and sensitivity. We all have such capacity. I had been able to experience our more diffuse - but no less fundamentally human - correspondences to the vegetal world on pensive walks in my local forest. I was examining at the same time my own footprint as an architect and the confused, exploitative foundations of the ideologies and histories the profession carried forwards, sometimes without really thinking about where it was going. I was entering into Richard Powers' 'plant consciousness' through the daily pattern of reading, looking, thinking, walking and writing. At the same time, I was healing myself, connecting to a vaster world in which we are profoundly at home, but which we tend not to see. A world which - because we can find it other, alien, uncontrollable - some of us have tended to want to erase.

In late summer, several of this book's protagonists and inspiring forces gathered for a visit at our house in Southern Burgundy. Bruno Latour and his wife Chantal, Terra Forma co-author Alexandra Arènes and her partner Soheil Hajmirbaba, animal-oriented and wood-inspired architect Patrick Bouchain, delta-loving sociologist Emmanuel Duperrex and philosopher of animals Vinciane Despret filled the house and attendant ballroom with laughter and music rivalling the Mbutis for its endurance and intensity. Donna Haraway, the great and hilarious muse of human-canine companionship, would also have been with us, but for COVID-related travel restrictions.

All of these thinkers of the non-human world very sympathetically engaged with our canine co-habitant Suki, seen earlier enacting feats of foundational divination, assisting me to situate my Hardelot Elizabethan Theatre in its woodland setting. Suki, however, was not her normal self. She generally took her hostessing duties very seriously, chivvying guests along, making sure all their beds were comfortable, vocalising her approval in a sort of Mbuti-song that was achingly close to speech: just missing a few consonants to actually say what was so obviously meant: I love you, you are welcome here. And don't take yourself too seriously. She hid out in our room, rather timid, and made a sortie to enjoy the final day of a conference in the wooded gardens of the Chateau d'Huringy with the gang, hearing impromptu lessons from Latour seated on a Sequoia stump, staring at trapeze artist Chloé Moglia who illustrated Bouchain's talk about risk in education by hanging from a pine tree above our heads.

It would be her last comfortable day.

Over the succeeding three weeks, my wife and I found ourselves engaged in a desperate process of attempted empathy, trying to decrypt the various uncharacteristic signs of distress she was manifesting. It was agonising, and impossible: there are limits between us and our non-human friends, and we lived these limits intensely and tragically. It was a dreadful shock. Just before her semi-hosting the Latour gang, she had been bounding up the slopes of one of her favourite places, the dense larch forests of Val Ferret on the Italian side of Mont Blanc. Finding a remnant snow patch in the intense summer heat, she would throw herself down it headfirst on her back, legs wiggling joyously in the air. She was full of beans at the end of the day; we were exhausted wrecks.

There was, however, a premonitory gloom to that occasion: a very very large snow patch (in the form of the Planpincieux Glacier), looming just above our hotel, had frozen its streams in a sudden cold snap, and when the heat ramped up, the streams didn't flow again. There was a great fear of the build-up of a glacial lake which could detach the leading mass of the glacier - some 250,000 cubic metres - and destroy the fragile inhabitations in the valley below. I descended to the Hotel Miravalle bar late one evening to find the staff staring in silence at their portable screens, each bearing a red cross on a white background. It was not a cultish ceremony. They were reading emergency notifications from the Italian Red Cross ordering them to evacuate their establishment; in fact, the whole valley was being closed down early the following morning. We went from joyous forest-yompers to climate refugees in a few hours, and had to abrogate our communion with this extraordinary place, one of the very few unspoilt, unexploited, barely-commercialised forest landscapes in the epicentre of Europe. The climate crisis was unfolding right in the middle of things, amputating human settlements, threatening immediate disaster.

Suki - I realised, as she agonised and lost her motility - had been my guide throughout the thinking and writing of this book, my intermediary to the unfamiliar time and space of the forest. She has led me - as at Hardelot - to see the wooded world differently, from lower down, with heightened attention and a combination of senses, isolating sounds, mapping through smell, remaining alert to many other life-forms sharing the space. She would luxuriate in the long grass at the forest edge, hopping like a lamb, thrilling at the sheer pleasure of being in vegetation higher than her tiny (but supremely agile) body. She also gave chase to a wild boar several times her size, and started (until we intervened) an altercation with a snake. During the early stages of the Coronavirus lockdown she became our legal forest guide: we had to carry a signed affidavit permitting ourselves to go outside for the essential purpose of walking our dog. She thought it was great, that humans had finally figured out that life should be simple, repetitive and celebratory.

During the lockdown she also - through her enthusiasm and insistence - led us to discover something hiding in plain sight, something to which we had never paid particular attention before: the daily bursting energy, the utter vibration, the clamorous transition, the forcing of vertical life from the ground towards the sky, that is early spring in a temperate deciduous woodland. Had we looked even closer, we would also have seen insects metamorphosing, juddering, fighting backwards and forwards between two seemingly irreconcilable states.

All births and deaths are - like this - transitions of a certain violence, marked by exclamations, spilt body fluids, and a shuddering reaction to a most profound change in the order of the world. Her own death - when it came - was no different. We howled - like dogs - and, feeling a strong compulsion, paced very fast through the forest as the dawn broke, emerging on a fang of rock which surveyed the Cluny valley, scene of global gatherings of knowledge a thousand years before.

We received - in her memory - a vast flow of tributes. She had already officially entered architectural history, her divination antics documented and credited in the concrete-dusty pages of the construction industry bible *Le Moniteur*. One of the most moving tributes came from Vinciane Despret. She had noted - during our jolly gathering - that the Coronavirus was bad for humans, but had protected birds. All was not symmetrical. In cities - where we bugger up avian territoriality with our noisy vehicles and such like - the virus lockdown had been a marvellous opportunity for our feathered companions to repossess urban sonic space and figure things out better amongst themselves. There were myriad other examples of the non-human world flourishing in our temporary absence. Vinciane had also profoundly understood the bonds and territory we shared with Suki.

In her tribute she cited psychoanalyst Jean Allouch's notion that the departed do not leave by themselves, as distinct entities. Rather - besides their physical bodies - they disappear with a co-constructed identity, part them, part you. In our case - with Suki having lovingly policed our marriage for ten years, during some of which time I was a bit like Dante, lost in my own midlife forest - this intersection was triangular. We each had our own missing part, but there was also another ripped-out entity, common to all three of us.

This shared part is the interself. It is the hardest to lose, and it is also - whilst we have and can cherish it - the most vital, the most earthly of conditions. *No man is an island* - and no dog or tree neither. The pain I must cross having lost loved ones - human and non-human - is the price of the mystery and joy of the interself. This joy is no different to - and utterly proportional to - the great love we can feel for the whole world which accepts and welcomes us. And the forest is the greatest interself, the foundation, the beating heart, the lung, the frame, the armature of thought and dreams, of ourselves and all animated things.

My father's story did not entirely end in the grave with my mother in Gloucestershire. We took a small part of his ashes and buried them in the roots of the fig tree in our courtyard garden. He had a special relationship with Suki: she reserved one of her most spectacular greetings for him alone, even though she only saw him about once a year. Her ashes now rest with his.

And the fig grows, itself an interself. Swells. Gives forth. Trembles. Will die in its turn.

Acknowledgements

The idea for this book germinated from a lecture given to the students of Bruno Latour, Frédérique Aït-Touati and Emanuele Coccia at SPEAP-Sciences Po. It grew - as a tree does in a forest - alone, but alongside them, mysteriously nourished from below by a shared network of understanding, inspiration and support. Making final revisions, I had to change references to Latour from the present to the past tense, feeling rather like an axeman or executioner. He was the biggest and most generous tree in the forest, and the maintenance and propagation of his root-matter is now a distributed affair, a shared entreprise, in which this book is one early new growth among many to come.

Other mighty trees - also nourishers of the present volume - fell at the same time: Peter Brook, Christopher Rådlund and the apex-forester Elizabeth II. As did my parents-in-law Bernard and Mary Catherine O'Rourke, whose barn woodshop in Pennsylvania was the starting-point of my own journey towards craftsmanship and the capacity to act on the world with my own hands.

My father's death spurred the nascent idea of the book in a new direction, focused on the questions of sharing, awareness and continuity; by dying, he became a particular protagonist. In many ways this is a book about families, whether biological, tribal or affiliate. Amongst these, my wife Bridget O'Rourke was - as always - a primary interlocutor, and the text has been further chewed over, pruned, and fertilised by Allison Selwood Catanzaro, Tess Thomson, Derek Thomson, Sarah Jarsbo, Clem Crosby, Polly Gould, Shawn Evans, Ron Henderson, Ted Landrum, Lisa Landrum, Stine Ilum, Hermann Kaufmann, Vinciane Despret, Malina Duta and - with particular dedication and attention - Fiachra Gibbons and Melissa van Drie. I am grateful to Kim Locke (NASA) for directing me to documentary resources relating to deforestation.

The two Japan-centred chapters of this book benefitted immensely from my 2015 residency at the Villa Kujoyama in Kyoto, and from the generosity and insight of several friends from that time: Haruhito Sano, Kengo Kuma, Diane Josse, Pierre-Jean Giloux, Manuel Tardits, Benoit Jacquet, Kibo and Yuki Hagino and Akira Kikuchi

Flemming Wisler, Hans Ulrik Gerdes, Laura Benedicte Petersen, Christian Snæland and Stine Skøtt Olesen of NXT and Nybrogade Press have created fine conditions of soil, water and air for the book to sprout, grow and stand proud in the forest.

Selected Bibliography

Aït-Touati, Frédérique et al.,
Terra Forma, Manuel de Cartographies Potentielles
(2019, Paris, B42)

Aït-Touati, Frédérique and Coccia, Emanuele (dirs.),
Le Cri de Gaia, Penser la Terre Avec Bruno Latour
(2021, Paris, La Découverte)

Ashmole, Philip and Myrtle,
St Helena and Ascension Island: a Natural History
(2000 Oswestry, Anthony Nelson)

Banker, James, *Piero della Francesca, Artist and Man*
(2014, Oxford, Oxford university Press)

Barber, Daniel,
Modern Architecture and Climate, Design Before Air Conditioning
(2020, Princeton, Princeton University Press)

Bardon, Jonathan, *The Plantation of Ulster,* Gill Books (London),
2012

Barthes, Roland, *Mythologies* (trans. Lavers, Annette)
(1972, London, Jonathan Cape)

Bertelli, Carlo and Maetzke, Anne Maria,
The Legend of the True Cross in the Church of San Francesco in Arezzo
(2001, Turin, Skira)

Bonin, Philippe, Masatsugu, Nishida, Shigemi, Inaga (dirs.)
Vocabulaire de la Spatialité Japonaise (2014, Paris, CNRS)

Bouchain, Patrick, *Permis de* Faire
(2017, Paris, Editions Cité de l'Architecture)

Brook, Peter, *The Empty Space*
(1996, New York, Touchstone)

Buck, Stephanie, *'The first American settlers cut down millions of trees to deliberately engineer climate change,'* (2017, Timineline. com), retrieved April 3rd 2023

Chamberlain, Basil Hall (trans.), *Kojiki*
(1932, Kobe, J. L. Thomson and co.)

Cisar-Erlach, Artur, *The Flavours of Wood*
(2019, New York, Abrams Press)

Coccia, Emanuele *Filosofia della Casa* (2021, Turin, Einaudi)
Coccia, Emanuele, *The Life of Plants, a Metaphysics of Mixture*
(2019, Cambridge, Polity)
Coccia, Emanuele, Albert, Bruce et al., *Trees* (Exhibition Catalogue) (2019, Fondation Cartier)

Cronon, William,
Changes in the Land: Indians, Colonists and the Ecology of New England
(1983, New York, Hill and Wang)

Deakin, Roger, *Wildwood, a Journey Through Trees*
(2008, London, Penguin)

Delas, David, *Arbres et Arbustes en Campagne*
(2019, Arles, Actes Sud)

Descola, Philippe, *Une Ecologie des Relations*
(2019, Paris, CNRS)
Descola, Philippe, *Par-delà Nature et Culture*
(2005, Paris, Gallimard)
Descola, Philippe, *La Composition des Mondes*
(2014, Paris, Flammarion)

Duperrex, Mathieu, *Voyages en Sol Incertain*
(2019, Paris, Wildproject)

Frey, Pierre, *Viollet-le-Duc et la Montagne*
(1993, Grenoble, Glénat)
Frey, Pierre, *Viollet-le-Duc et le Massif du Mont Blanc* (1988, Lausanne, Payot)

Guenin, Hélène (dir.), *Sublime, Les Tremblements du Monde*
(2106, Metz, Centre Pompidou)

Hallé, Francis, *La Vie des Arbres* (2019, Montrouge, Bayard)
Hallé, Francis, *Le Bon Usage des Arbres* (2011, Arles, Actes Sud)

Harrison, Robert Pogue, *Forests, The Shadow of Civilisation*
(1992, Chicago, University of Chicago Press)

Haskel, David George,
The Forest Unseen, A Year's Watch in Nature
(2012, New York, Penguin)
Haskel, David George,
The Songs of Trees, Stories From Nature's Great Connectors
(2017, New York, Penguin)

Heathcoate, Edwin, *Imre Makovecz, The Wings of the Soul*
(1997, Chichester, Academy Editions)

Hofmeister, Sandra (ed.), *Timber Structures in Vorarlberg*
(2019, Munich, Detail)

Hoskins, W. G., *The Making of the English Landscape*
(1955, Harmondsworth, Penguin)

Houdart, Sophie and Minato, Chihiro,
Kuma Kengo, Une Monographie Décalée
(2009, Paris, Donner Lieu)

Hudert, Markus (ed.),
Rethinking Wood: Future Dimensions of Timber Assembly
(2019, Basel, Birkhauser)

Illich, Ivan, *H2O and the Waters of Forgetfulness*
(1986, London, Marion Boyars Publishers)

Isaacson, Walter, *Leonardo da Vinci*
(2017, London, Simon and Schuster)

Isozaki, Arata, *Japan-ness in Architecture*
(2011, Cambridge, MIT Press)

Jacquet, Benoit, Matsuzaki, Teruaki, Tardits, Manuel,
Le Charpentier et l'Architecte
(2019, Lausanne, Presses Polytechniques et Universitaires)

Kapfinger, Otto (ed.), *Hermann Kaufmann Wood Works*
(2009, Vienna, Springer)

Kikuchi, Akira, *'La Glocalisation de la Protection du Patrimoine
Folklorique : l'Exemple des Coutumes Liées à la Riziculture dans le
Nord de la Péninsule de Noto'*
(2015, Ebisu 52)

Koch Piettre , Renée, et al, *Mémoires de la Terre*
(2019, Grenoble, Editions Jérome Million)

Kohn, Edouardo, How Forests Think,
Toward an Anthropology Beyond the Human
(2013, Berkeley, University of California Press)

Kuma, Kengo, *Small Architecture, Natural Architecture*
(2015, London, Architectural Association)

Latour, Bruno, *Down to Earth: Politics in the New Climatic Regime*
(2018, Cambridge, Polity Press)
Latour, Bruno, *Où Suis-Je? Leçons du Confinement à L'usage des
Terrestres* (2021, Paris, Editions de la Découverte)
Latour, Bruno, *Où Atterrir? Comment S'orienter en Politique*
(2017, Paris, Editions de la Découverte)
Latour, Bruno, *We Have Never Been Modern*
(1993, Cambridge, Harvard University Press)
Latour, Bruno and Weibel, Peter (eds.), *Critical Zones: The Science
and Politics of Landing on Earth* (2020, Karlsruhe, ZKM)
Latour, Bruno and Schultz, Nikolaj, *Mémo sur la Nouvelle Classe
Ecologique* (2022, Paris, Editions de la Découverte)

Laugier, Marc-Antoine, *Essai sur l'Architecture* (1775, Paris)

Lewis, Simon and Maslin, Mark,
'Defining the Anthropocene' in *Nature 519*, March 11 2015

Macé, Marielle, *Nos Cabanes* (2019, Lagrasse, Verdier)

Macfarlane, Robert, *Underland* (2019, New York, W. W. Norton)

Maloof, Joan, *Teaching the Trees, Lessons From the Forest* (2007,
Athens, University of Georgia Press)
Maloof, Joan, *Nature's Temples, the Complex World of Old-Growth
Forests* (2016, Portland, Timber Press)

Mayo, Joseph,
Solid Wood, Case Studies in Mass Timber Architecture
(2015, London, Routledge)

Montelle, Edith and Domont, Philippe,
Histoires d'Arbres, des Sciences aux Contes
(2014, Paris, Delachaux et Nestlé)

Moorehead, Alan, *Darwin and the* Beagle
(1978, Harmondsworth, Penguin)

Morgan, Morris H. (trans.),
Vitruvius, the Ten Books of Architecture (1960, London, Dover)

Nakamura, Yoïchi, 'Mori tu Bunmei o Kangaeru,' in
Shinto Bunka Kai (ed.), *Shizen to shinto bunka 2: Ki/Hi/tsuchi*,
9-31 (2009, Tokyo, Kobundo)

Natterrer, Julius, et al., *Construire en Bois*
(1994, Lausanne, Presses Polytechniques et Universitaires Romandes)

Pallasmaa, Juhani, *The Eyes of the Skin, Architecture and the Senses*
(2005, London, John Wiley)
Pallasmaa, Juhani, *Animal Architecture,*
(1995, Suomen Rakennustaiteen Museo, Helsinki)

Panofsky, Erwin, *Perspective as Symbolic Form*
(1991, Brooklyn, Zone)

Petit, Jean (dir.), *Un Couvent de Le Corbusier*
(1961, Paris, Les Editions de Minuit)

Powers, Richard, *The Overstory*
(2018, New York, W. W. Norton)

Rackham, Oliver, *Trees and Woodland in the British Landscape*
(1990, London, Orion)

Rahm, Philippe, *Histoire Naturelle de l'Architecture*
(2020, Paris, Adagp)

Ritchie, Ian (ed.), Todd, Andrew (contributor),
Neuro Architecture, Designing With the Mind in Mind
(2020, London, Architectural Design / Wiley) incl. article 'Plant
Consciousness, Towards an Architecture of Expanded Kinship'

Rots, Aiki P., *Shinto, Nature and Ideology in Contemporary Japan,
Making Sacred Forests* (2017, London, Bloomsbury)

Rykwert, Joseph, On Adam's House in Paradise
(1981, Cambridge, MIT Press)

Shakespeare, William, et al (trans.)
The Authorised King James Bible
(2008, Oxford University Press)

Slovic, Scott et al., *Routledge Handbook of Ecocriticism and Environmental Communication*
(2019, Abingdon, Routledge)

Thorsen, Line Marie, *Moving Plants*
(2017, Naestved, Ronnebaeksholm)

Todd, Andrew, 'Les Arbres, Qui Nous Abritent, Sont des Etres
Politiques' (28.4.2021, Paris, Le Monde (editorial))
Todd, Andrew, 'Kengo Kuma,' Sustainable Design 5, Vers Une
Nouvelle Ethique Pour l'Architecture et la Ville, Revedin and
Contal (Eds.), Alternatives/Cité de l'Architecture, Paris,
2017. pp 124-128.

Todd, Andrew, 'Akira Kuzumi, Superstar Plaster Craftsman,'
2016, published on www.studioandrewtodd.com/thinking
Todd, Andrew, 'Kengo Kuma, Killed by Concrete,' 2018 published on www.studioandrewtodd.com/thinking
Todd, Andrew, 'Sotigui Kouyaté Obituary' (The Guardian
2.5.2010)

Tsing, Anna Lowenhaupt,
The Mushroom at the End of the World
(2015, Princeton, Princeton University Press)

Turnbull, Colin, *The Forest People*
(2015, London, The Bodley Head)
Turnbull, Colin, *The Mountain People*
(1972, New York, Simon and Schuster)

Vasari, Giorgio, *The Lives of the Artists*
(trans. Bondanella, Julia and Peter)
(2008, Oxford University Press)

Viollet-le-Duc, Eugène-Emmanuel, *Entretiens sur l'Architecture*
(1858-1870, Paris, Morel)
Viollet-le-Duc, Eugène-Emmanuel, *Histoire de l'habitation humaine depuis les temps préhistoriques jusqu'à nos jours*
(1875, Paris, Hetzel)

Wilkinson, David and Smith, Humphrey, *'An Initial Account
of the Terrestrial Protozoa of Ascension Island,'* in Acta Protozool
(2005, London)

Wilkinson, David, *'The Parable of Green Mountain: Ascension
island, Ecosystem Construction and Ecological Fitting,'* in Journal of
Biogeography (2004).

Wohlleben, Peter, *The Hidden Life of Trees*
(2016, London, Harper Collins)

Zürcher, Ernst, *Les Arbres, Entre Visible et Invisible*
(2016, Arles, Actes Sud)